The Section 8 Bible

Section 8 Housing Guide

*"How my partner and I carved out a nice living
in a not-so-nice neighborhood."*

D1736148

Michael McLean
Nick Cipriano

For Mom and Dad,
whose unfailing support for all my schemes and
dreams underlies each and every page of this book.

For the late Henrietta MacNamarra,
Nick's Mom,
whose strength and soul
have made Nick the man he is today.

CONTENTS

PREFACE

Before you read this book, I might be able to save you some time. If you don't have the following three items, you're not going to succeed in this business, therefore, don't buy this book:

#1 Common Sense

#2 Good credit

#3 Balls – you'll need them!

Also, I will let you know this up front, this book is strictly based on protecting the landlord, saving him money, and ridding himself of nuisance tenants. I will be the first to tell you that some of the things you read in this book concerning treatment of tenants may seem harsh. However, they are all surefire ways to save money and succeed in this business.

WHAT THIS BOOK IS

This is a true, unfiltered story of our accomplishments, failures, and experiences as Section 8 landlords over the past 8 years. Nothing is held back. You get the good, the bad and the ugly, told in a raw yet understandable way. There are no lawyers saying, "You can't say that," nor ghostwriters saying, "Say it like this." Everything you will be reading is something that Nick and I have experienced firsthand and have written down in our own words. Some writings may motivate you, some may deter you, some you will learn from and some you will laugh at. All you will find interesting, that we guarantee.

WHAT THIS BOOK IS NOT

This book is like no other because it is not a manual filled with junk to buy to help make you a great Section 8 landlord. We are not trying to sell you leases, products, CDs, seminars or "systems." We are strictly giving you information on how to purchase real estate and then how to make money while renting your property to a Section 8 tenant. Leases, products, and "systems" can't make you rich. The only thing that can make you rich is determination, and that comes from within. You're the only person who can make yourself rich. Getting up early in the morning and working late 6 or 7 nights a week while applying the information in this book may or may not make you rich. But it sure as hell is gonna help!

I've read other books on Section 8 real estate rentals and I have literally gotten sick to my stomach. Nobody told the truth about the ugly side of the tenants or the Section 8 program. Nobody gave specific tips on how to pass inspections or how to get around some of the ridiculous Section 8 rules. But we will! I've read hundreds of books telling you what you *need* in your Section 8 rentals to pass inspection. Nobody has ever given detailed lists of what to eliminate from your Section 8 rentals because you *do not need* it to pass inspection. But we will! Items such as garbage disposals, dishwashers, ceiling fans, etc. If they are in your property and don't work or stop working, you will fail your inspection. If you eliminate them before your tenant moves in, you will pass and continue to pass your inspections.

Most books or guides on Section 8 only tell you the upside to the program. Why? They want you to purchase the book. They don't want to scare you away. Never will they tell you about any of their nightmares. But we will! Not only will we tell you about them, we will tell you about what you can do to prevent them! Nobody else will even touched on the subject of how to go about keeping yourself safe while working on your properties. Let's face it, sometimes you're going to be working in some "not so desirable" neighborhoods. Why would these other books not even make mention of this? Once again, they don't want to scare you away. They don't even want you to think about the negatives let alone mention the dangers. But we will!

We are going to tell you everything we know about being a Section 8 landlord. You're going to understand everything we are saying and every point we are making. No sugar coatings or big fancy words. We think you'll appreciate it. Most importantly, when you put this book down, you're going to have a pretty good idea of if you want to become a Section 8 landlord or not! Whether you choose or choose not to, if we have given you valuable information, then we feel as though we have done our job.

If you are thinking about throwing your hat into the Section 8 housing ring, you have purchased the right book. We have placed in your hands the best book ever written on the Section 8 rental business. It is now up to you to choose what you want to do with it!

INTRODUCTION

My name is Michael McLean and I am the author of this book. My partner and coauthor is Nick Cipriano. We are both in our thirties and have known each other since we went to elementary school together. We were raised in a small suburb just ten minutes from Southwest Philadelphia called Sharon Hill, Pennsylvania. It was in this section of Philadelphia where Nick and I went to work.

From 1997 to 2004 we purchased, repaired, and rented out over 300 homes. Ninety-nine percent of the homes we rented were to low income families. Along the way we gathered valuable knowledge, all of which I intend to pass along to you. This is something I think you must know. Between the two of us we only came into this game with $34,000. Not much money, but we both had something as valuable as money, a burning desire to be wealthy. Here's how it all got started.

After graduating high school in 1984, I took a job as a maintenance man in a 400-unit apartment complex in Philadelphia. I didn't really know much, but I knew that I had the common sense to pick it up on the job. I ended up staying with this job for 10 years. Along the way, I learned some valuable knowledge of simple, basic fixes. The bigger jobs, such as HVAC, service panels, and sewer line replacements were all subbed out to contractors. Other things such as installation of locks, toilets, stoves, floors, outlets, light fixtures, painting, etc. were all part of my basic everyday duties.

After working at this position for 10 years, a close friend of mine had pulled some strings and got me into the laborers' union. This position paid a lot better and provided better medical benefits. However, I must admit, this work was ten times harder than what I was used to. But, oh well, you gotta go where the money is! It didn't take long for my first unlucky break in this field. While into my second week on the job, I fell off a 30 yard dumpster and broke the L1 vertebrae in my back. The injury sounds worse than what it was, however, I was not able to return to this position. I suffered no permanent injuries but remained on workman's compensation for 2 years due to weakness in my lower back. After 2 years I was bought out by the insurance company for $34,000. After the lawyer took his 20%, I was left with $28,000.

After receiving my settlement, it was time to get back to work. The only thing that I knew was maintenance, so I answered several ads in the local paper. Within one week, I was hired as a maintenance manager of a property consisting of 120 units.

I still had $28,000 and knew I wanted to build some type of business with it. But what? What could I put my money into that, if it didn't work out, I could sell the business and/or materials and recoup some of my losses? Real estate was the answer! I knew that stocks and bonds could fail, but real estate was just as it sounded, "real" You can see it, you can touch it and you can be proud to say you're the owner of it! But how? How was I going to buy property with only $28,000? And where? Where could you buy property this cheap?

I remembered a friend of my brother's telling me that his mother had died and he was selling her house. He only wanted $18,000 for it because it needed work and it was on a small street in the city. After kicking this idea around for about a week, I decided to give him a call. He told me to meet him at the property on Saturday morning. When I arrived, I was already too late. His brother had sold the house to a local investor for $14,000. An Agreement of Sale had been signed and there was nothing he could do.

Getting into my truck I was disgusted. Disgusted at myself for not pulling the trigger on this deal a week sooner, disgusted and thinking I may not get another shot at a handyman special so cheap. It was while pulling off the street that a break came my way. I noticed in a window of a house on the street a 'For Sale by Owner' sign. I wasn't going to wait this time. I parked my truck and called the number on my cell phone. The owner of the home lived around the corner and said he could be there in 10 minutes. Within a half an hour of my phone call, we had a deal for $10,000 ($4,000 lower than my brother's friend's house) and a signed Agreement of Sale. Finally, I was in business.

After officially taking possession of the house in July of 1997, I began working on it on the weekends and every night after leaving my job at the apartment complex. I was excited and looked forward to getting there and completing the project. After three weeks it was ready to be rented. I ran an ad in the local Philadelphia paper and had over

100 phone calls. About 60% of these calls were from people saying they had Section 8 packets. I was not familiar with this program, so I bypassed all Section 8 callers. This was mistake #1!

A local minister had called me and told me he had the $550 rent and $550 security deposit. He wanted to move into the property by August 1st. Great, I thought!

On August 1st, I met the preacher at the house. He told me he came up $150 short because he had to help somebody out at his church. He said, "Don't worry. If you give me the keys today, I will have your $150 by the 3rd." I was anxious to get the property rented and took him at his word. Mistake #2.

I'll tell you this – I never received another dollar from the so-called preacher. Turned out, I was dealing with the devil. I didn't know the first thing about how to get him the hell out of my house. Eviction was a foreign word to me. I did know that this was eating me up. Eating me up because I couldn't kick down the door to my house and drag him out by his throat. He had rights, I was told. In any other industry, if you are using someone's product without paying for it, it's called stealing. If you don't pay your gas, phone or electric, they shut it off. If you don't pay your car payment, they repossess it. But in real estate, you have to pay money to get someone thrown out. That's just the way it is.

By the beginning of September, I received my 2nd break. The police had raided the preacher's house (my goddamn house) and arrested him on robbery charges. I wasted no time taking repossession of my property. The preacher only had several pieces of furniture and two bags of clothes. One of the officers told me he wouldn't need the clothes where he was going. He would be issued an orange jumpsuit with numbers on the back. I took great pleasure in driving his furniture and clothes to the local dump. Something else had also happened. I now had a bad taste in my mouth about the real estate world. I no longer wanted to be a part of it. After owning the home for only 2 months, it was now back up for sale. I went to the local hardware store and bought a 'For Sale' sign identical to the one that was in the window when I bought the house. After pulling up to my house, I noticed the man that had bought my brother's friend's house doing work on it. I thought that if he had paid $14,000 for one on the same street, he would certainly buy mine for the $10,000 that I had paid. I knocked on the door and we began to talk.

He laughed when I told him that I had had it with the real estate game. He said he would certainly buy the house for $10,000 but he had a question. "Why are you selling it?"

I told him, "I didn't feel like getting beat for rent ever again."

"Have you ever heard of Section 8?" he replied.

"Yes, but I'm not quite sure what it is."

"It's a government program in which the tenant lives in the house and the government pays the rent. It's the only way that I would rent a home."

So, I decided to try again. I was either nuts, stupid, or deep down, I still had a burning desire to succeed in this business. Anyway, I was back in the ring and ready to take another swing.

Once again, I ran an ad for a house for rent and received many phone calls. This time I bypassed the private industry and only accepted the Section 8 calls. After gathering information on Section 8 housing, I rented the house to a Section 8 tenant on October 1, 1997. Now I will only I rent a home to a Section 8 tenant in a low-income area. I receive my rent on-time, every time. It worked out so well that on November 15, 1997, I purchased my second rental property for $14,000. By December 1st, 15 days after the purchase, this house was up and rented to a Section 8 tenant. That made two on the payroll.

If you're good at math, I guess by now you figured out that I had very little capital left. The two properties had cost me $24,000. Renovation and closing costs had eaten up the remaining $4,000 of my $28,000 settlement, leaving me with a fat zero in my savings account. However, I was quite happy with adding a guaranteed $1,350 to my monthly income. The first house I purchased rented for $700 per month and the second rented for $650 a month. But now I had a dilemma. I craved real estate and was sick to my stomach whenever a good deal passed by, and many did. I had to figure out a way to get my hands on more money to close these deals, but how? Where? That's when my phone rang!

"Hello, Mike. What's up? It's Nick."

"Yo, what's goin' on Nick?"

"Ah, nothin' much," he replied. "But, listen, I was talking with Wayne and he told me you own two properties and they are both rented out Section 8."

"Yeah," I said.

"How's that working out for you?" he asked.

"Not bad, not bad," I said.

"Cool, listen. I know where we can get a house for $14,000 if you want to go in on it with me."

Now, to be honest with you, I really wasn't ready for that question. Like I said, I had known Nick since second grade and we hung out with each other occasionally until we were about 20 years old. We talked to each other on occasion about twice a year, but we had mutual friends who filled us in on what the other one was up to. I knew that at one time Nick had owned about 15 homes in the area, but that he and his partner had split and sold off the properties. He was now living in a factory which was converted into his house. The upstairs, where he lived, was huge. The downstairs was made into a gym on one side and a storage warehouse on the other.

He told me to stop by, lift some weights, and bullshit about going into business together. After I arrived, we got a quick workout in and it was now time to sit down and talk business. I did not know if he was as serious about the real estate field as I was, but I was willing to listen to what he had to say. I also had several questions for him such as why his previous partnership had ended, what was his knowledge of repairing homes, what kind of money did he have to invest, and most importantly, how far did he want to go with this.

I knew within five minutes of talking that he was just as serious, if not more serious, than I. He had told me that his old partner had not wanted to put out any money to expand the business. Nick wanted to continue to buy homes, tools, supplies, etc. Once he told me this, I knew we were both on the same page. As for Nick's knowledge of repairs, it turned out he knew more than me. He was very strong in the electrical field, but he brought something more to the table. He knew people, lots of people in different fields – plumbers, electricians, roofers, painter's, handymen, etc. If we couldn't do the repair, Nick knew someone who could. And the best part was they all worked fairly cheap and reasonable. Most of these guys had full-time jobs but would come up to the city at night or on the weekends to do side jobs. They all appreciated the extra cash.

I told Nick everything sounded great and that I would love to go in on a house with him, but there's only one problem.

One huge problem.

"What's that?" he asked.

"MONEY! I'm broke!" I said.

"Really? What about credit cards?"

"How the hell am I going to buy a house with a credit card?" I said, laughing.

"Take a cash advance!" (I will cover more about credit cards in Chapter 2).

"Is that what you're doing?" I asked.

"No, not yet. Right now, I have enough for this house. But on the next one, I'll be doing the same thing as you."

I thought about it for about 10 seconds and figured, what the hell. My half of the rent would surely cover the minimum payment on a credit card, and besides, with two of us in on the house, the cost of repairs would be cut in half and the project would get done twice as fast. On January 10, 1998, it was official. I had my third rental property and Nick and I became partners!

After completing the repairs on this home in the record time of 1 week, we had the home rented and on the payroll by February 1st. Two more purchases quickly followed. Both of these homes were also purchased with credit cards. We were now both starting to get excited about the potential of our business. We worked Monday night through Thursday night (Friday nights off) and Saturday and Sunday nearly all day. I can honestly say we never argued with each other and never bitched about the work. In fact, we **enjoyed** it. We were our own boss. No one was looking over our shoulders telling us to hurry up. If we went to lunch for two hours, oh well! When we felt like calling it a day, that was it, nobody standing there telling you it's not 5 o'clock yet. It got to the point where I didn't want to do this just at night and on the weekends. I wanted this life every day. I promised myself that when I got the monthly rents up to my monthly salary, I was gone! Outta there!

On February 16, 1998, the sixth house was purchased. It was a Friday, we weren't working that night, so I decided to stop over Nick's house to see what was on the agenda for the next morning. When I arrived, Nick was sitting in a side room of the house which at the time was being used for our office. Behind him, hanging on the wall, were two 10" × 8' neatly painted black boards. Each board had 50 hooks, 25 on the top and 25 on the bottom. Attached to each hook was a blank key chain. On the first six hooks were the keys to the homes we already owned. My eyes nearly popped out of my head.

"What the hell is that!" I laughed.

Nick, getting right to the point, returned, "It's a keyboard and we're going to fill it. You gotta think big, Mike, because when I do something, I don't do it small or half-assed. We will fill this board in 3 years, I guarantee it!"

Turns out, he was wrong, we did it in 30 months! And, oh yeah, we filled four more boards just for good measure. By the time we decided we owned enough homes, we had over 300 rentals!

Now comes the good part, the reason you bought the book! We're going to tell you how we did it, and how you can do it. We're going to tell you several different ways to get the money to buy your first home – after that first purchase, the rest get easier and easier to acquire. We're not going to tell you the bullshit in these other real estate books like 'let the seller pay your down payment and closing costs' or 'have the seller give you a 10% seller assist.' None of that, because in 99% of these situations, it does not work. The deal usually blows up before it gets to the table or, if the seller is smart, he'll tell you thanks but no thanks. The only thing that works all the time, every time is cash. And, we're going to tell you how to get it. Granted, our way may be riskier than begging a seller to give you some of his money, but like I told you in the beginning, if you don't have balls, then don't buy the book.

We're going to walk you through all the steps of getting your house rented with a government program, whether it's Section 8, Track, Transitional Housing, we'll have you passing inspections the first time the inspector comes out. We'll show you where to find tenants, how to get them in your home and how to begin getting paid for the property.

We're going to show you the quickest way to complete your renovation projects and, more importantly, how to save thousands in getting it done. We will literally give you over 200 tips throughout this book and every individual tip will save you at least five times more than what you paid for this book. I don't care if you own 1,000 homes, you will still find something in this book that's going to save you more than what you paid for it.

So, here we go, let's get started on the purchase of your first property. If you already own properties, then let's get started saving you some cash!

CHAPTER 1

SECTION 8

What is Section 8 and how does it work? Also, learn how to screen your prospective tenant.

Section 8 is a government program created to help low income families pay their rent. In some instances, all of the rent is paid; in others, a portion of the tenant's rent is paid and the tenant is responsible for the remainder. In most cases, the family is also given a utility check. This enables them to pay their electric, gas, water, etc.

Here is how it works. A family who is having trouble keeping up with rent payments or who are homeless and living in a shelter apply for housing assistance. If they are chosen for the program, they must report to their nearest housing office to be evaluated. The evaluation considers their background, criminal record, income, number of children, etc. If the family passes all qualifications, they are put on a waiting list to receive a housing voucher.

The packet or voucher goes by bedroom number. The higher the number of bedrooms, the more the landlord can ask in rent. The bigger the family, the higher the number of bedrooms, since there is generally a max of 2 people per room. Plus, adults must sleep separate from children and boys must be separate from girls.

Example: An elderly woman with no children would be issued a one bedroom packet. A single mother with one child would be issued a two bedroom packet. A single mother of 2 boys, again, would be issued a two bedroom packet. A family made up of a mother, boy and girl would be issued a three bedroom voucher. In some areas children under 5 may sleep with their siblings regardless of gender. It's easy to figure out, the more children, the bigger the packet size. Most importantly, the bigger the packet size, the more rent you will receive.

Once the family has the packet in their possession, they will begin to search for a home to rent. If they choose your home, they must give you their packet in order for you to fill it out. Once you are in possession of the packet, this is what you want to do.

Screening Your Tenant

Ask the tenant for her phone number and present address. Tell her you will call her when you are done filling the packet out and you can arrange to set up a time and a place to meet with her so you can return it to her. However, you will not be calling her; you are going to show up at her present address *unexpectedly* to return the packet. Simply tell her you were in the neighborhood and thought you would save her a trip. Tell her the last thing you need to do to qualify her is to take a quick look through the house she is presently living in. If she denies you access, simply deny her from renting your house. If she doesn't want you to see inside, she's obviously hiding something: bad housekeeping, a pet, illegal tenants, whatever the case may be. If she's wrecking the place she's in now, yours is next. If her home is not too bad and you don't see a lot of damages, then rent her your home. Don't get too carried away and break out the white gloves for inspection. After all, it's a rental property and you don't have to sleep there. Your investment is not making any money while vacant.

This is the only background check that I perform on my prospective tenant. Section 8 does a pretty good job of screening the tenants before they are entered into the system. A criminal background check is performed so at the very least, you won't be renting to a felon. What a background check will never show is how well a tenant is going to take care of your property. It's a gamble but so is everything else in life. Even if you rent to an exterminator, it doesn't guarantee you'll get your property back without roaches in it.

Some people like to do credit checks, but I feel it's a waste of time. Ninety percent of the time the rent is being paid by Section 8 so that eliminates the tenant from paying. When we began this business, we started performing credit checks, but we would have to go through about 100 people just to try and find someone with o*kay credit.* At $35 per credit check, you can see where this would get expensive. Even if you had the future tenant pay the $35, it's still time consuming and most of the people in the program simply do not have good credit. Nobody who has bad credit is going to throw away $35 to be told something they already know. The solution is simple, get more security money. You may think, well, OK, if somebody needs help paying rent, how are they going to come up with a large security deposit? Well, you'll be glad to know that there are several different agencies who help people in the program with security deposits. So, get as much as you can out of them before they take possession of the property. Too much security is never a bad thing.

Another background check landlords like wasting their time on is calling the tenant's present landlord. Forget it! This procedure usually works in reverse. If a landlord called me and wanted information about a *bad* tenant of mine, I would tell him that she is the greatest tenant in the world. "Boy, I'm really gonna miss her." Little would he know I would be doing back flips and he would be adopting an asshole tenant of mine. If a landlord called and asked me about a *good* tenant of mine, I would be hesitant to giving him information on just how good a tenant she was. The reason is simple, I wouldn't want to see her go. Don't waste your time calling other landlords. You won't know if you're getting the truth or lies.

Back to the packet! After you return the packet to the tenant, they will return it to Section 8. Section 8 will then call you and set up an inspection date. You must be present for the inspection. Once you meet the inspector at the property, he or she will inspect the home. You will either pass or fail. If you fail, the inspector will write out a list of repairs that must be completed. After completing these repairs, the inspector will return to re-inspect. If you pass, he or she will give you a rating from 1 to 9, 1 being the worst and 9 being the best. This rating is based on several things such as condition of house, location and amenities. This score will factor into what your rent will be on the property.

The inspector will bring your inspection report back to the Section 8 main office. If the property passed, the report will be sent to appraisals. The appraiser will then determine the rent. If the "fair market" (average rent) for a three bedroom house is $750 in a particular neighborhood and your inspection rating was average, your rent would most likely come in at $750. If it was less than average, you would receive less and if it was above average you would receive more.

So now let's say your rent is determined to be $750 a month. Section 8 will call to notify you when you and your tenant can come in to sign the lease. After your leases are signed, you receive a copy, the tenant receives a copy, and Section 8 keeps a copy. The Payments Department processes your lease and your home is now, as we like to say, "on the payroll." You will be paid the first of every month. Section 8 in Philadelphia has direct deposit. You will need to fill out a form to sign up for direct deposit

Your property will be inspected annually. If your property passes inspection you will continue to get paid, but only temporarily. If your property fails inspection, you will have 30 days to perform the required repairs. That's what this book is all about, passing inspections and eliminating future repairs.

CHAPTER 2

START UP MONEY

GETTING THE MONEY TO GET STARTED

Over the years many people have asked me, "How did you get started and where did you get the money to buy all those houses?" Well, now I am going to let the cat out of the bag, you only need to find enough money to buy one! After the first one, the rest fall into place, and in this section, I'm gonna show you how. But first things first. Let's work on getting you that capital to close your first deal.

The first and most important thing is cash. When trying to hash out a deal on a property, cash is your number one bargaining chip. It enables you to get the deal done quickly and without any hassles. You can make it to the settlement table in 30 days or less with cash! When taking a mortgage, it could be 60 to 90 days before sitting down at the table. It cuts out the middleman. Who is the middleman you ask? The mortgage company or bank! Nobody enjoys dealing with them whether you're the seller or the buyer. So, I'm going to show you how to come to the table with cash in hand. A very important thing was said to us years ago, and I'll never forget it.

A realtor who had sold us several houses called us up to look at some properties. He knew we had been buying a lot of homes and he asked, "How many homes are you guys up to now?"

"About 40," Nick replied.

The realtor grinned and said, "I'm not impressed with bricks, it's cash. Cash is the only thing I'm impressed by." Nick and I laughed, but we always remembered it because it's true. You can have 1,000 houses, but if they're not rented or you're getting beat for rent, then the only things you have is bricks!

The fastest, easiest, and least expensive way to get the money you need is by borrowing money against your primary residence with a home equity loan. Most banks charge zero points and usually you'll find this to be a very low interest rate. When taking a home equity loan, always be sure that your monthly rental income is going to be double what your monthly home equity payment equals.

Here's an example. Let's say the property you wish to purchase costs $24,000 and it needs $4,000 worth of repairs. This total comes to $28,0000 so you decide to take a $30,000 home equity loan. The loan is for 10 years and is at 6%. Your monthly payment would be $340. The rent you should receive would be $680. Anything higher than this would be icing on the cake. An easy way to find out what a home would rent for on a certain street is by simply asking Section 8. Call the Appraisals Department and ask what the "average rental" is on a 2, 3,

4, etc. bedroom home on the street on which you wish to purchase.

After you have taken the home equity loan and purchased your investment, the investment property is now free and clear of mortgage. Your primary mortgage has a home equity loan attached to it, but nothing is owed on your investment piece. This now becomes "untapped monies." If you decide that you want to purchase another property, you can borrow against your rental property. You can either take a home equity loan on this property or do what is called a "cash out." They are both very similar and, in most cases, a bank will give you 75% to 80% Loan to Value (LTV). The bank will appraise your rental property, tell you what it's worth, and then you may borrow 75% to 80% of this number.

When calling around to different banks for rates, here is what you should ask. "Hello, my name is John Dough. I would like to know what your rates and LTVs are for home equity loans."

The banker will ask you for how many years. Tell them you would like a quote on both a 10 and 15 year loan. Sometimes a bank will be running a special rate on one or the other. And always, get a fixed rate mortgage. If the rates go up, yours won't. If the rates go down, you can always refinance.

The same holds true in taking a cash out or home equity on your rental property. Make sure that the home you are purchasing will rent out for double of what your monthly payment is. This is how you get your volume or number of houses up. Every time you pull money out of one to buy another, the one you purchase is free and clear of a mortgage. This now becomes your next source of money. The process keeps repeating itself until you are satisfied with the number of rentals you own.

Another way to get the money you need to make a purchase is with credit cards. I have purchased several homes this way when I was first starting out. I know this may sound risky but first, hear me out.

Many credit card companies will send you cash advance checks offering you different incentives to use them. I've seen deals such as "no cash advance fee" and "1.99% for six months." Whatever the case may be, look for the best possible deals that you can get and apply for the card. The ones with the larger credit lines of say, $10,000 to $15,000 usually run the best deals. Once you receive your credit cards, be sure they come with cash advance checks. If they don't, simply call the credit card company and have them send them out to you. Once you have your deal in place and are ready to close on it, simply fill out the checks (made out to yourself) and deposit them in your checking account. Once the money is in your account, you will need to go to the bank and ask for a "cashier's check" for the amount you will need to close the deal.

Sounds a little risky, huh? Well first of all, you're not going to keep the balance on the credit cards very long. The minute the property has been repaired and rented out, you will be calling the banks and telling them that you have a property you wish to take a loan on. Since you used credit cards to purchase the property, the property is free and clear of debt. You can borrow up to 70% or 80% of what it is worth. You might even be able to stick some cash in your pocket before even renting the house out.

Cost of home:	$22,000
Cost of Repairs:	$ 4,000
Closing Costs:	+$ 2,000
Total:	$28,000

Now let's say the property appraises out at $45,000 after you have completed the repairs. Now let's say the bank will let you borrow up to 75% of its value.

House appraisal:	$45,000
Bank LTV rate:	75%
Money borrowed:	$33,750
Money spent:	-$28,000 → this pays off the credit card
Money in your pocket:	$ 5,750

And, by the way, that $5,750 is tax free. Uncle Sam gets none of it! You can either put it in your pocket or, if you're smart, put it towards your next investment. It will be $5,750 less that you have to borrow. If you do 5 deals similar to this, you should end up putting about $28,750 ($5,750 × 5 = $28,750) in your pocket. Now you will be using your own money rather than credit cards to make your next purchase.

A third way to get the money you need to make a purchase is through hard money lenders or "B" lenders. Their interest rates are higher, but they are much more creative than a regular bank. Banks have strict guidelines that they have to follow. "B" lenders make their own guidelines. You can find them in your local phone book in the Yellow Pages. They will be in the loan section, usually using a name such as *Blank* Finance Company. The word 'finance' as opposed to 'bank' is usually a good clue that you are using a "B" lender, in most cases. Also, in this book, we will tell you who we used.

Some of these companies will give you the money for your purchase, the money for repairs, and the money for closing. You come to the table with nothing more than a pen. And, get ready to use it because you will be papers until your hand is ready to fall off. But one paper you better **not** sign is the one saying you do not have the option to pay the loan off early. Don't get trapped in a loan with a high interest rate. Make sure there is **no** prepayment penalty. What this means is, if you decide to pay off the loan early, the finance company can charge you astronomical fees. Some finance companies have prepayment penalties, some don't. It's about 50/50. Call around until you find one that does not. It shouldn't take long to find one.

Now, naturally if you borrowed from a finance company and they gave you the money for the purchase, closing, and repairs, they are also going to give you some high fees and a high interest rate to boot. First let's talk about the fees.

The first thing they are going to get you with is the points. What is a point? A point is 1% of the total loan. So, let's say you were taking a loan for $100,000; 1% of this loan would be $1,000. If the bank were charging you 3 points, your total would be $3,000. If you were borrowing from a bank or "A" lender, your usual loan would consist of anywhere from 0 to 3 points. But when borrowing from a "B" lender, it can be anywhere from 1 to 8 points. They will also get you for appraisal fees, document preparation fees, participation fees, etc. Anything to get the loan total up higher. Depending on how strong your deal is, you can usually negotiate with them.

How do I know if I have a strong deal or not? Simple – if the total amount of money you are borrowing is 20% lower than what the property appraises for, then you have a strong deal. Example: If the property is worth $100,000 and the total amount you wish to borrow is $80,000, then you are only borrowing up to 80% of what the property is worth. The lower you go, such as borrowing 30% or 40% lower than what the property appraises for, then the stronger your deal becomes.

A finance company, as well as a bank, will be more willing to lend on a property knowing that if they have to foreclose on it, they will be able to sell off the property for a profit. No bank or finance company wants a property to end up back in their lap, but if they know that the property is worth more than what they are lending you, there is zero risk of them losing a nickel. They will be more willing to maybe lower the points involved and/or the interest rate. Even some of the other fees may be lowered or removed from your loan.

Your credit score will also play a vital part in your negotiations. The better the score, the better the negotiations. The worse the score, and well, you know the rest.

The point I'm trying to get across here is the more risk you are going to be putting the finance company at, the higher your fees and rates will be.

What can I do to lower the risk? If you are going to be using a finance company, you have to shop. Shop and search for a house that will be at least 20% under appraised value when complete. This does not mean going out and buy a house that is in need of tons of repairs because it is priced at 20% lower than all the other homes in the neighborhood. You must figure your repair cost into your final figure.

Example of a weak deal:

House price:	$ 80,000
Cost of repairs:	$ 15,000
Total house costs:	$ 95,000
Comparable home value:	$100,000
Loan to value:	95%

Example of a strong deal:

House price:	$ 55,000
Cost of repairs:	$ 10,000
Total house costs:	$ 65,000
Comparable home value:	$100,000
Loan to value:	65%

You are now 35% under the Loan to Value. The finance company is not at risk. You should be able to negotiate a nice deal. The more you are under appraised value, the better off you are. You want the chips on your side of the table, not theirs. Believe me, if you shop around enough, you'll find the right house. They are out there.

Blanket Mortgages: What are they? Can they save me money? What are they for? Do all banks have them? I will answer all these question in this section. I will even give you the three banks we used who specialize in this type of lending.

#1. What is a blanket mortgage?

Let's say you have been purchasing properties for 2 years now. You buy six properties a year and now have 12 properties. You have 3 loans with one bank, 3 with another, and 2 loans with three other banks. The reason you have so many loans is because most banks will only give you three to four loans and then you have to search for another bank who may give you two or three loans. Now you have several different banks and several different loans. Any easy way to keep better track of your payments is to consolidate all your mortgages into one. If you are like me and like to stay organized with your finances, it's the best way to do it. When you take all your loans and consolidate them into one, this is called a *blanket mortgage.*

#2. What are blanket mortgages for?

Like I just said, they really keep you organized. But that's not it! When you take a blanket mortgage, the bank you are taking it from will be paying off all your existing bank loans. Now you can go back to these banks that you paid off and try to open a credit line or, once again, use them for 2 or 3 mortgages on your future deals. You now have their trust because you paid them in full. They will be happy to do business with you again. It opens you up to them again, so to speak. Also, after paying off a couple of these banks, your credit scores will begin to rise through the roof, giving you leverage when negotiating your next deal.

#3. Can a blanket mortgage save me money?

Absolutely! Here's how. Let's say the 10 homes you are going to be consolidating have a total balance of $800,000. Now you want to find your average interest rate. It's easy. Get out your mortgage documents for all 10 existing loans that you have. Each one will have an interest rate. First you multiply each balance by its interest rate.

Loan A balance x Loan A interest = A
Loan B balance x Loan B interest = B
Loan C balance x Loan C interest = C
Loan D balance x Loan D interest = D

A + B + C + D = yearly interest payment

Then you add all those numbers together. The last step is to divide by your total balance owed.

Loan A is $80,000 at 8%   = 6,400
Loan B is $110,000 at 9%   = 9,900
Loan C is $120,000 at 7%   = 8,400
Loan D is $90,000 at 7%   = 6,300
Loan E is $40,000 at 6.5%   = 2,600
Loan F is $80,000 at 7%   = 5,600

Loan G is $90,000 at 8%   = 7,200

Loan H is $65,000 at 8%   = 5,200

Loan I is $75,00 at 8%   = 6,000

Loan J is $50,000 at 8%   = 4,000

Total: 61,600

61,600 / 800,000 = 7.7 %

Your average interest rate is 7.7%. When you sit down to negotiate your deal with the banker, try to cut 1.5% off your interest rate. Why would a banker want to give you a lower rate right off the bat? Because of the size or amount of the deal. If you throw 9 to 10 houses into one deal, that deal is going to be pretty sizable, even if you are dealing with $80,000 investment pieces. A bank might have to do 5 or 6 separate loans to equal the amount of the loan you are handing them. Also, the collateral should be pretty good considering you are throwing several homes into the mix. And remember, when doing a loan like this, a bank can be pretty creative also. You should be able to get them down in points, interest rates, and fees. The bigger the loan is going to be, the sharper their pencils will get.

#4. Do all banks do blanket mortgages?

No, and here is why. If you have 5 properties that you would like to take loans on, most banks would rather you take 5 different loans. The reason is simple. Fees! They would rather charge you document prep fees, wiring fees, credit check fees, etc. five times instead of just once, as it would be in a blanket mortgage. If you plan on keeping your properties for the life of the loan, a blanket mortgage is simply the best way to go.

You may have to shop around for a while before finding a bank who carries blanket mortgages. There are many out there that do and I'm sure you will have luck in finding one. In the next chapter, I am going to list 3 Philadelphia area banks who specialize in this type of lending. I am also going to list one finance company that I would recommend.

CHAPTER 3

BANKS AND LENDERS

Throughout my years in the real estate business, I have dealt with many banks, some good, some bad, and some that were terrific. Luckily for you, I'm going to spare you the bad.

In this chapter, I am going to give you the names and numbers of the only banks that I will deal with. I will also give you a contact name. I will tell you what the bank specializes in, how they might start you out, and my personal opinion of them. Like I said in the beginning of this chapter, I won't give you the bad ones so what you're going to read about the following people and their banks is all good. You will enjoy doing business with them.

Port Richmond Savings Bank

2522 East Allegheny Ave

Philadelphia, PA

Contact:

Tom Werynski, Vice President

(215) 634-7000

Offers blanket mortgages, single family and investor loans. For Philadelphia-based investors only.

Port Richmond Savings Bank is *a bank,* so you will need good credit. A credit score of over 650 should get your foot in the door. You will also need your last 2 or 3 years of tax returns. Depending upon your credit score and history in the real estate field, you should be able to take a 70 to 75% loan to value loan on your property. Port Richmond also offers Blanket loans. All loans are usually about 3 points with very fair fees.

Tom Werynski is the man you will be dealing with and I've never met a more honest or fairer banker. From day one, Tom never has reneged on a deal, added on unnecessary extra fees, or been late getting a deal to the table. If Tom gives you his word on something getting done, count on it, it's done! His word really means something. The speed of the loan is what we really enjoyed. Port Richmond has a board meeting the first Tuesday of every month. If you get your application in before that meeting, then 90% of the time you will be settling your loan before the end of the month!

Now, let me tell you something else about Tom and Port Richmond Savings. If Tom says your rate is 7%, it's 7%. Don't waste your time trying to get it down to 6.9% because it ain't gonna happen. The rates are fair and competitive to begin with. Also, if your loan application is denied, you're not going to be able to talk yourself into a loan. If Tom can help you and you qualify, he will help you. If he can't he'll waste no time telling you so.

Tioga Franklin Savings Bank

320 E Girard Ave

Philadelphia, PA 19125

Contact:

Bob Lockyer

(215) 423-8012

Offers blanket mortgages, single family and investor loans.

Tioga Franklin is also *a bank*, so, once again, you will need good credit and probably your last 2 or 3 years tax returns. Tioga Franklin has similar lending patterns as Port Richmond Savings Bank, but your credit line maximum will be smaller (probably around $300,000) Again, your points will be about 3 and the fees will be fair. Your loan to value at Tioga Franklin can reach as high as 80%.

The man you will be dealing with is Bob Locklear. I didn't deal with Bob for very long because we paid his bank off pretty quickly. What I can tell you is that the 9 or 10 times I had to use his bank, he came through for me. The loan was done on time and the fees were low. I don't know if you can talk your way into a lower rate or lower fees because I did not deal with Bob over a long period of time. What I do know is that they are an honest, fair and well-organized bank. They are also a bank you can count on.

> Republic First Bank
> 1608 Walnut Street
> Philadelphia, PA 19103
> Contact:
> Mark Kane, Vice President
> (215) 735-4422
> Offers blanket mortgages, single family and investor loans.

Republic First Bank is a very aggressive bank. They want your business. All of your business – and they will do what it takes to get it. This is a bank where truly the more you come in with (property, excellent credit scores, years in the real estate field, collateral, etc.) the better deal you will leave with. However, if you don't have all of the above, you're still not out of luck. They will try to put you in a deal that works for both of you.

The man you will be dealing with is Mark Kane. Mark is a hustler. I don't mean hustler in a bad way, for if he were, I wouldn't recommend him. I'm talking about a guy who is always trying to put together a deal. The bigger, the better. If he can't put together a deal for you, he'll ask you if your brother owns any property. As far as credit lines go, I don't know where his start or end. I've done two blanket loans through Republic First Bank which totaled over 4 million dollars and I'm quite sure that if I brought him in another million dollar deal tomorrow, he would find a home for it by day's end. It also helps that we have had an excellent relationship with his bank since day one. No late payments, no lapse in insurance coverage, no excuses! We make business easy for him and he makes business easy for us – the way it should be.

Republic First Bank's interest rates are competitive, and their fees are low. If you have a deal worked out with another bank, it wouldn't hurt to run it by Mark. If you're looking for a guy with a sharp pencil, you'll find none sharper than his. If he says he can beat your deal, take him at his word – he'll beat it.

Stonehedge Funding, LLC

Contact:

Jim Bennett, President

(610) 873-6022

Offers blanket mortgages, single family and investor loans. For Philadelphia-based investors only.

Stonehedge Funding is not a bank, so they can get very creative. I wouldn't say they are a hard money lender or a "B" lender. I would put them in the middle of the two. I usually don't like to use or recommend finance companies because their rates and fees can get pretty high. I'll tell you straight up, Stonehedge Funding's fees and rates can get pretty high also, but read a little bit further and you'll see why I recommend using them. You'll also see what type of buyer should use them.

The man you will be dealing with is Jim Bennett. Within two minutes of talking to Jim, you'll find out that this guy knows a lot. He knows a lot about lending and he knows a lot about investor loans. This is what his company specializes in. How does he know so much about what's on both sides of the fence? Because Jim started out as an investor. A Section 8 landlord! In fact, he began investing in the same Southwest Philadelphia neighborhood as Nick and I and he still owns homes in this part of the city.

Jim was sharp enough to come up with an idea on how to lend money to other investors in the area to get them where they wanted to go. Nick and I were two of those investors.

After maxing out our credit lines at Port Richmond Savings and Tioga Franklin Savings Bank, we now had to begin shopping for a new bank. Meanwhile, deals on properties were still being offered to us. We needed money to close these deals quickly before somebody else stepped in. That's when I was recommended to Jim Bennett.

Talk about getting the money quick! After hashing out a deal with Stonehedge Funding, we closed on our property in only 6 days. Everything at Stonehedge is done in house including the appraisals. This is why they are able to move so fast on a deal. It worked out so well that we did approximately 20 deals there. The rates and fees are, of course, higher than a bank, but there are no prepayment penalties. Once we found a bank that gave us another credit line (Republic First), we were able to refinance the loans we had with Stonehedge Funding to a lower rate with Republic First Bank. Although Stonehedge Funding is not a bank, you still can get yourself a better deal with good credit. Stonehedge has several types of loans, including the type that will pay for your purchase, closing fees, and repair costs. I know that Jim has grown his business much larger since the last time we used them and now offers more products. I have found them to be very honest and the <u>only</u> secondary lender I would recommend. You can also look up their website at www.stonehedgefunding.com.

MY FINAL THOUGHT ON START-UP MONEY

The bottom line is this, you want to get yourself into a position where you are using the bank's money. You want the banks call and ask, "Hey, would you like us to increase your credit line?" The only way to do this is by establishing a relationship with a bank, using the same bank for the same type of loan over and over again. I recommend always make your payments 10 days early rather than on the first.

For the investor that is just starting out, your path will be a little riskier. Credit cards, finance companies, and home equity loans are a little bit trickier, but you must do what it takes to get that first piece of property under your belt. Once you own about 4 or 5 pieces of property, you won't have to go searching for a bank – the bank will find you!

CHAPTER 4

THE TURNOVER

GETTING YOUR PROPERTY READY
FOR SECTION 8 INSPECTION

The turnover and getting your property ready for a Section 8 inspection go hand in hand, therefore, I am combining these sections into one. I will tell you what you have to install or eliminate during the turnover so that you will pass the Section 8 inspection. I will go into detail of the exact products we used in our homes and where to purchase them. We will cover every product we used from the roof to the basement floor. We will cover every field: plumbing, electrical, roofing, painting, flooring, etc. By the time you're done reading this section, you will see how easy it is to pass a Section 8 inspection and you will see how much easier it is to save money while doing so.

Before we get down to business, do you remember when I told you that some parts of this book may seem harsh? Okay, well it's about to start getting harsh. Throughout the years of being in this business, you learn how to repair things. When your repair something and it breaks again, you scratch your head and think of a better way to repair it. After you read this chapter you will no longer have to worry about scratching your head and thinking of a better way to repair things. Nick and I have come up with a surefire way to only repair things once. It's called **elimination** and it works on just about everything: screen doors, closet doors, door knobs, carpet, outlets, exhaust fans, etc.

Here's how it works. For some reason the same objects in all of our rental properties would end up broken. The majority of the time it was screen doors and closet doors.

We would move a tenant in to the home and after about 2 or 3 months that call would come. "Mike, my screen door is broken!"

"What's wrong with it?" I would ask.

The handle broke off, or the screen got ripped or the closer doesn't work – always something. It got to the point where we were losing our minds. One woman's door broke 3 times in a 2-week period. First, the screen ripped, then it wouldn't shut right, then the handle fell off. Well, she finally caught Nick on the wrong day. After hanging up the phone, I asked who it was. He told me it was the lady that didn't know how to take care of her screen door, so he was going to go over and take care of it for her. When he returned, he had the door in the bed of his pick-up truck. The six-month-old door looked like it was 60 years old. Nick threw it in the trash.

The woman called back about 20 minutes later and asked Nick if he was repairing or replacing the door. "Neither. You don't know how to take care of a screen door, so you don't get one anymore!" Nick snapped back.

We called Section 8 and asked if you needed a screen door to pass inspection. Whatta ya know, a screen door is considered an amenity and you don't need one to pass inspection! From here on out, it was easy. If we bought a house that had a screen door, we would leave it on. The first time a tenant called about a problem with a screen door, we would tell them to fix it themselves or we would remove it.

This technique worked so well that Nick came up with another brilliant idea. He suggested we get a copy of the Section 8 rule book. The rule book in Philadelphia is called the book of <u>Housing Quality Standards</u> or better known as <u>HQS</u>. These rules are very similar in most states. Anyway, if something was not in the rule or code book and we didn't need it to pass inspection, it was gone! It's like going into a car dealership and getting the 'stripped down' economy version – roll down windows, manual transmission, no radio, no A/C, no power locks, no power steering, etc. The less that you give 'em, the less they have to break. The less they have to break, the easier the inspection is to pass. Get the idea?

If not, we're going to tell you what to eliminate and why. Always remember this when you are eliminating something from your property. **It's a rental property!** You are not fixing the property up for resale and you are not fixing it up to live in. You're getting it ready to pass a low-income housing inspection. You're eliminating a problem before it becomes a problem. It's called preventive maintenance, or as we like to say, "very preventive maintenance." Maybe you've heard the saying, "if it ain't broke, don't fix it." Well, how about "if it ain't there to break, you'll never have to fix it!" There are about a thousand things that you can remove from your rental property and all will save you cash. Lots of cash! So, let's get started on how to begin your rental property turnover.

CHAPTER 5

THE CLEAN-OUT

Before starting your clean-out, you will need to make a list of everything that you want to eliminate from your property. Take a walk through the property and make a decision if an item is staying or going. Obviously, you will be removing all the trash from the property but there are many more objects in the home on which you have to make a decision on such as carpets, vanities, sink bases, light fixtures, etc. Some of these items could be expensive to replace in the beginning but may end up saving you money in the long run. In our "Elimination" chapter, we will cover everything in the home that should be eliminated and when to eliminate it. When you are writing your clean-out list, you will know exactly what to remove. Your clean-out will not be complete until each and every object that you wanted to eliminate is crossed off of the list.

A lot of times in this business, you buy a property with the clause of "as is" condition. That is exactly what it means. The way you looked at it when you made your offer is the way it is going to look when you make your settlement. In some cases an elderly person has died and all their belongings remain in the property. In other cases, a bank forecloses on a property and the family that was living in the property takes their valuable possessions and leaves behind their trash and junk. In spite of that, this is how you will be taking possession of the property. There are only two ways to remove the rubbish from the home. There is the expensive way and the inexpensive way, but both are very simple. Let's get the expensive way covered first.

Pick up the phone book and call three different "clean out" companies. Show them what you want out of the property and get their price. Take the lowest price and wait until they finish all the work. I never pay until a job is complete. If somebody tells me they need two or three hundred dollars to get started, then they are not much of a business man. Move on to the next guy that does not need a deposit. Pay them, and the clean-out part of your project is done. But I guarantee you this, if you call someone out of the phone book, you're going to pay at least triple the amount as what it would cost you to do it yourself.

Doing it yourself: I'll give you two ways; one if you own a pick-up truck and one if you don't. If you own a pick-up truck, it will make things a lot easier, but if you don't you can still get the job done.

First you will need trash cans and plenty of them. We recommend you use the Brute Cans with handles on the side. These cans are carried by Home Depot and I am sure if you look around, you can find them at any major department store. Using the cans is more efficient and quicker than just throwing trash into the bed of your truck. You can get at least twice as much trash loaded into the cans than by just throwing trash into the bed of the truck. It saves you time while you are in the house by not having to run back and forth with two or three pieces of trash. Simply pack the can as full as you can get them and then drag or carry them out to the truck. Once you get about 12 cans (most 6' beds will hold 10 cans, 8' beds should hold 14 cans) start stacking them neatly and tightly onto the back of your truck. Now that your truck is full, where will you be taking it?

Once again you will need your local yellow pages. The words you will be looking up are recycling services or recycling centers. All should accept trash and rubbish and there should definitely be a center within 5 miles of your home. Find the one that is closest to you and go there and dump your trash. By neatly placing your rubbish into cans, this will save you valuable time when dumping. Simply take the cans off the truck and dump them. Had you thrown the trash in the bed without the cans, it would have taken much longer to unload it.

If you do not have a pick-up truck, your next idea would be to get a dumpster delivered to your job site (rental property). The dumpsters come in various sizes and there is no time limit on them. The company will charge you by size only. Once you fill the dumpster, the company you chose will come back out and remove it. Here are the typical prices: 10 yard for $350, 20 yard for $490, 30 yard for $620, and 40 yard for $780. This is not a bad way to go, however, sometimes the city will make you get a permit to place the dumpster in front of the house. Also, you will get a lot of complaints from the neighbors about the dumpster clogging up the parking on the street.

Clean-out tip:

After everything that was on your list is removed, go from room to room, wall to wall and remove all screws, nails, picture hooks, curtain rods, etc. This is one less thing you will have to do before painting the unit.

Final thought on clean-outs:

When Nick and I first started out, we both owned a pick-up truck. Between the two trucks we were able to get a minimum of at least 20 cans of rubbish to the dump per trip. Clean-outs are a dirty job, but they must get done. Not only must they get done, they must get done first. Start your project out on the right foot and do the clean-out properly. Make sure that everything you wanted to get rid of in the house is gone before you move on to the next step. If you purchase a home that is loaded with furniture and trash, the minute you finish ridding yourself of it and broom sweeping out the house, you will notice a huge difference. You will actually see what you have to work with and what it will take to complete your project. It will also make your next task (the renovation checklist) easier to write.

After Nick and I reached the 40 house point, we purchased a stake body. We bought it used for $5,500 and we still use it today. It makes quick work of clean-outs. Simply pack the bed as full as you can get it, take it to the dump, remove the gates, hit the dump button, and you're gone. I wouldn't recommend getting a stake body if you are just going to be purchasing a couple of homes. If your intentions are larger, then a stake body is a must have vehicle for your business. I'm sorry we didn't purchase it at the 10 house point. It would have saved a lot of time and effort.

Our stake body truck

CHAPTER 6

CONTRACTOR REPAIR LIST

This is the list you will be writing first. It's a list of outside contractors that you will be bringing into the home and a list of repairs you want them to complete. We have two handymen who work for us full time and handle all of the basic repairs in our homes. For the more complicated repairs, we use outside vendors who are skilled in one specific field. The contractors we use are a roofer, electrician, plumber, heater technician and carpet installer. You might be thinking, "Why don't they hire a handyman who could do all of these things? Wouldn't it be cheaper and quicker to get the property turned over?" Well, I'm sure everybody has heard the phrase, "Jack of all trades, master of none." That would be the answer to your question.

Most of the time, having your handyman handle these five things is not any cheaper, nor does the property get turned over any faster. Bringing in a skilled craftsman for a specific job will be quicker, and in the long run, it should be cheaper. Most importantly the job will get done correctly. Not only does it get done correctly, but in most cases, you get a guarantee. If a roofer puts on a rubber roof and you get a 5-year warranty, any time it leaks just call him back. If a plumber puts in a new vertical stack and it leaks, call him back. If your carpet installer installs new carpet and it starts to buckle, call him back. But the best part of using somebody who knows exactly what they're doing is most of the time you won't get any callbacks.

Let's say I had my two handymen putting on a roof and I'm paying them each $100 per day. They are up on the roof for 4 days – I just spent $800, not to mention what it would cost for supplies. Their trade is not roofing so, of course, they're going to be slower than a seasoned roofer, and I'm sure their quality of work won't be the same. Now that they were up on the roof for 4 days, I am 4 days behind on the interior repairs that need to get done. Had I hired a roofer from the very beginning to install the roof for $1,000 (average price for a rubber roof on a rowhome) I would have gotten a warranty, quality work, been four days ahead of schedule and, if you add in material, I probably would have saved a couple of bucks to boot! Let the roofers roof, let the plumbers plumb, let the... you get the point!

Here's what you and each of your contractors should check.

Roofer's checklist: It does not really matter what order you get your other 3 contractors into the property, just as long as you get your roofer in first and your carpet installer last. The reason for this is simple. Any painting or materials that are in the home will be ruined if your roof is bad and it rains. Once the property is sealed from water, begin your interior work.

The reason the carpet goes down last is common sense. Your painters don't have to waste their time with drop covers if there are no carpets on the floor. Also, if there is no carpet down, your workers can't have any accidents like tracking mud in on them or spilling a soda on them. If anybody has an accident on the carpets, let it be the tenants. At least they have a security deposit you can deduct from.

Naturally, the first thing your roofer will be checking is the upper roof. Also, if you have a front porch and/or back porch roof, he will also have to check them. You should be able to get a good idea of what kind of condition your roof is in just by looking at the interior upstairs ceilings. If you see heavy damage, chances are you will be needing a new roof. If you see some small water stains, you may only need a coating.

Here's a tip: try to stay with the same roofer. We have kept the same roofer from day one. It makes it so much easier if a tenant calls to tell you about a leak. Rather than trying to think back who did the roof or look up the info on it, simply just call the guy that has done every one of your roofs. Besides, he will have a better idea what's going on up there since he's the one that did the work. You will develop a business relationship with this person, and you will have a pretty good idea of what he charges for each job (new roofs, coatings, downspouts, etc.) Also, you will begin to trust him as long as your roofs are not leaking.

If he comes off the roof and tells you it needs a new roof, he's going to give you two choices, rubber or tar. **Never choose tar!** Rubber will last as long as you own the property. All you have to do is coat it about every 5 years and it will stay in good shape. Tar roofs start to blister very early on, and no way will they last you as long as a rubber roof. You will be spending about $200 more for rubber but it's well worth the investment.

If the roofer tells you the roof looks as though it's in good shape, have him throw a coating on it anyway. This way you know you're in good shape. A coating will only cost you $200 and you won't have to worry about any leaks for about 4 or 5 years. If you have a shingle roof and it's in good shape, leave it alone. If your roof needs to be re-shingled, check how many layers of shingling are already on the roof. If you only have one layer of shingles you may place your new shingles directly over the old ones. If there are 2 or more layers already on the roof, the roofer will have to perform a "rip off." This is when all the shingles are ripped off right down to the wood.

If you have a slag roof and it is not leaking, again, leave it alone. A slag roof is a roof covered in tiny stones. Many rowhomes years ago used this method of roofing, however, it is now obsolete. The first call you get from your tenant about the slag roof leaking, replace it. With these roofs it is hard to find where the leak is coming from, and besides, you already know it's old. Replacing slag roofs can get expensive because first all the stones have to be removed from the roof. Our roofer charges us $1,400 to remove a slag roof and replace it with rubber.

56

If your property has a skylight, have your roofer throw a coat of muck around the base of it. You should be able to inspect the condition of your skylight just by viewing it from inside the bathroom. If it's leaking, rusted to death and just doesn't work, you may have to have the roofer replace it. We get a new skylight installed for $225.

The last thing your roofer will be checking is the gutters and downspouts. Make sure they are clear and draining properly. Another thing you must check is if they have chipping or peeling paint on them. A downspout that's 10' or shorter can be painted with Rustoleum paint. Any downspout that is longer than 10' you should seriously think about replacing it rather than painting it. Some downspouts run 30' or longer so it would be more economical to change it rather than waste your time and money painting it.

Heater Technician checklist: Gas or Oil? Sometime before your tenant moves into the property you want to get the heater checked out to see that it's working properly. Sometimes the homes you purchase have been sitting vacant for a couple of years and rust or water damage may affect your heater. A heater technician will be able to fire your heater up and see if it's working properly, needs any repairs or parts, or if it just needs to be serviced (cleaned up, new filter, etc.) Again, you want to find somebody you can trust and build a business relationship with. You may get lucky and find that your plumber also does heating. In our case, our heater repairman just fixes heaters. He has worked for the Philadelphia Gas Department for 25 years fixing heaters and has had his own side business for 20 years fixing and installing heaters. We were very lucky to find him because not only was he knowledgeable, he is also reliable. As long as a tenant would call me before 4:00 pm to tell me she had no heat, he would be at her door by that night. He would be able to either get her temporary heat that night, have a part on the truck and fix the problem immediately, or tell her he would get the part in the morning and install it. This is the kind of guy you're looking for. Not the guy who you call on Tuesday and he gets to the property by Friday. Now you've got a tenant as well as Section 8 calling you for 3 days asking you when you're going to get your tenant some heat.

As far as our heater guy's knowledge of heaters, you couldn't get any better. As long as our heater is gas operated, not oil or steam, he could fix it. I don't care if it was 40 years old, he could over haul it and have it running like new. Ninety-nine percent of the other guys out there would look at it and tell you that you need a new heater. I would rather pay $300 or $400 to completely overhaul a heater than to pay $2000 to replace one. I'm not writing this paragraph to brag about our heater guy and say, "look what we found!" I'm simply telling you to look around for a guy that has a ton of knowledge and is very reliable. They are out there. You may have to weed through a couple of bad ones but they are out there!

All right, now I told you I would put $400 or even $500 out to save an old gas heater, right? I would not put out more than $100 to repair an oil heater. Anything less than $100, okay, fine, I'll deal with it and make the repair. Anything more than a $100 repair, I would invest the money towards putting in a new gas heater. Why? Because oil heat is nothing but problems. Here's why:

#1 Finding a repairman who fixes oil heaters is tough. Most of them don't even want to touch it, and if they do, they're gonna charge you good.

#2 They always break down. I don't know why, I'm not a heater technician. But, I can tell you this. Out of my 300 properties, only 17 had oil heaters. I got more calls on these 17 heaters than the other 283. That's no bullshit.

#3 And this is the kicker – the tenants! That's right – the tenants! If you have oil heat in your house, I'm sure you go down the basement to check if the needle is on a half tank or quarter tank. THEY DON'T! They will wait until they run out. They may call you or they may call for a delivery of oil. Either way, you're going to get involved. Here's why. Once the oil has been delivered and the oil truck leaves, the tenant still won't get any heat. They will pick up the phone, call you, tell you they just got a full tank of oil and the heater's still not working. When you ask them if they paid the delivery man $20 to prime the heater, the answer is always no. When your heater runs out of oil, it must be primed so that it will start sucking oil through the system again. The next sentence out of their mouth is going to be, "Why do I gotta pay for that – it's your heater?" Once again, it's time to put on the boxing gloves because you're about to go 10 rounds over the phone with a jackass who thinks it's your fault that *she* ran out of oil. This call became so common that I could tell you what they were going to say next. We finally got smart and put an addendum to the lease that says if *they* run out of oil, they're responsible for priming.

#4 You guessed it – tenants again! Although your heater may be run by oil, the stove is run by gas. What does the gas stove have to do with anything you ask? A lot! If a tenant runs out of oil and doesn't have 10 cents to their name, do you think they're going to freeze until they can afford some oil? No, they're going to walk over to the stove, throw all the burners on high blast, turn the oven up to 500° and open the oven door. Not only are they putting a hurtin' on your oven, they're risking burning your property down. How do I know? Because it happened to me.

I've owned hundreds of properties for over a decade now and have only had one fire. I guess I'm pretty lucky, but I believe you create your own luck. Had I changed the oil heater to gas, I wouldn't have had any fires at all!

I know that if you're just starting out in this business, you may not have $2,000 to put out for a gas heater right away. You need to repair things in the home that *don't* work before you replace something that does. Here's an angle you can try. Suppose when you are buying the property you get the seller down to $35,000. Take another look around the property and tell him you didn't realize the property had oil heat. Tell him the bank you're dealing with won't let you finance a rental property with oil heat because of the dangers it poses. Ask him if he would be willing to come down $2,000 off the price so you can replace the heater. The worst he can say is no. If he says yes, don't stick the $2,000 in your back pocket and consider yourself a shrewd negotiator. Stick it in your heater man's hand and tell him to line you up with a new heater. You will be glad you did. No heat calls for about 10 years is worth $2,000 to me, especially if someone else paid for the heater.

Plumber's checklist: Writing the plumber's check list will be different than the way you wrote the heater technicians and roofers list. You *tell* the roofer and heater tech what you want them to check for you. The plumber's check list you will write for them. The first room you will be inspecting is the bathroom. You're going to make decisions on the items you want to replace such as the toilet, vanity, tub, lavatory faucet, and tub diverter. The products we use and how we make the decision on if we are going to replace a certain item in the bathroom is explained in detail under **bathroom checklist.**

The next room you will be inspecting is the kitchen. You will be making decisions on if you are going to replace your kitchen sink, trap, or faucet. This is further explained in detail under **kitchen checklist.**

For the items you want the plumber to check, fix or eliminate in the basement, you will be reading one of the best chapters ever written on keeping water bills down. (Chapter 8)

Electrician's checklist: In each and every house we purchase, we have our electrician replace every outlet, switch, toggle plate, GFI and light fixture in the house. The outlets and switches go for 50¢ a piece. The GFI's go for $11 a piece. The toggle plates go for 50¢ a piece and the lights go for $9 a piece. Add up all the material and it will add up to about $125 per house. Spend $125 and you never get a call for electrical problems.

We always purchase the same lights, switches and outlets, so after your electrician does about 2 or 3 of your houses, it will be like a cookie cutter for him. He'll know exactly what you want done. Any and all ceiling fans are eliminated and replaced with a $9 light fixture. It doesn't matter if your ceiling fan is a Hampton Bay worth $150; replace it. The reason for this is simple. If you move a tenant into the property and it has a ceiling fan, when it breaks, what will they want? You got it, another ceiling fan. If you feel like you're wasting a perfectly good ceiling fan, don't. Take it home and hang it in your house. I guarantee (money back not included in this offer) that the ceiling fan will look better and last longer in your home.

Another thing we feel is necessary to eliminate is 220 lines, especially when the outlet falls under a window. The reason for this is so that your tenant does not put an air conditioner in the window. Not that I don't want my tenant to feel comfortable in the summer, but I would rather not have them install an air conditioner in the window. The reason for this is simple. Usually, the air conditioners the tenants hook up are old, gigantic, and weigh about 200 lbs. All three of these factors go against you.

#1. The A/C is old. If it's old, somehow, someway it will end up blowing fuses. What happens when a fuse blows? Your tenant calls.

#2. The A/C is gigantic. It may not fit into the window. That does not mean your tenant won't try to force it to fit. Usually the glass in the window ends up cracking or breaking. What happens when a window breaks? Your tenant calls.

#3. The A/C weighs 200 lbs. By some miracle, your tenant gets this behemoth size A/C into the window without breaking the glass. Now you have another problem. You've got 200 lbs. sitting on top of a vinyl window. Although the vinyl may be pretty strong, it's a good bet that it will be cracked or destroyed when the tenant takes the A/C out of the window.

Another reason you don't want an A/C in the window is for the possibility of a lawsuit. Should the A/C fall from an upstairs window hitting someone or someone's car below, you know who that person is coming after. You – or to be more specific, your insurance carrier. I'm not saying removing a 220 receptacle will work every time in your effort to keep them from installing an air conditioner, but most of the time it does. Not too many tenants are going to pay an electrician $200 or more to install a 220 line for them. They would rather ask you if you could get one installed for them. After reading what you just read, I'm sure you won't hesitate to tell them no.

We also have our electrician go to the basement and eliminate any useless wires. If you look up in the rafters in some of these old houses, you may see a thousand wires. Not all of them operate something. Some could have been from an old electric stove, someone could have run lights to an old bookshelf which has since been eliminated, whatever the case may be, if the wires are dead, your electrician will find them and eliminate them. The only wires you should have there are the wires you need there.

The last thing you want your electrician to check is the service wire. Be sure that it is not fraying and that the plastic jacket around it is not cracked. If it is, it will need to be replaced. Our electrician has been with us for quite a while, so he does this job for us rather cheaply ($150). Not only is it a dangerous job because you're playing with high voltage, but you're also, in most cases, standing on top of a 40' ladder. Don't be surprised if most electricians want to charge you $250 for a service wire. You can't and you won't pass the Section 8 inspection with a decayed service wire. Find the best price and get it done. After that, you should be in good shape for the next 20 years or so.

Carpet installer's checklist: This should be the easiest of all. Decide which rooms in the home are getting new carpet. Call your carpet installer out to measure how many yards you will be needing. And last, but not least, call him back when all work has been finished on the property. <u>Always</u> make sure the carpet is installed last.

When should you replace carpets? After reading our flooring and ceiling section, you will be able to make the right decision all the time, every time. I will also tell you this, you won't be calling the carpet installer very often. This section is filled with many money saving tips on how to get around spending money on carpets, carpets that may only last the duration of one bad tenant.

CHAPTER 7

CHECKLISTS

Before stating your turn-over you will write a checklist or list of repairs. The checklist will be as valuable to your job as blueprints are to an architect. They play a very important role in getting your project started and finished. No project is started without a checklist and no project is complete until the last repair is crossed off the list. Writing a detailed and organized list will save you valuable time as well as keep you aware of what needs to be done and what has already been completed. They are very easy to write and get easier with every purchase. This is because the more turnovers you do, the more you know what to look for. A complete repair list should take no more than 1 hour to complete. In this section we're going to tell you what to include on your checklists, how to arrange them, where to start them and where to finish them. Let's get started!

Writing a checklist: First you will need a pen and tablet. We always start our checklist in the front of the house and end the checklist in the rear or backyard of the home. The first thing you will be writing on your tablet is "Front." Here's how you will set it up.

Any repairs that you see in front of the unit you will write down.

What should you be looking for in the front of a house? The first thing you will be looking at in the front of a house is the condition of the concrete. Check to see if any curbs, sidewalks or steps need to be repaired or replaced. If so, write it down. If you have steps that are more than a total of 36" high, you're going to need a railing.

The next thing you will want to look at is your water cap, water vent cap, and gas cap. Make sure all three are there. If one or all are missing, they can be purchased at any local plumbing supply.

Brick pointing: If your home is of brick construction, be sure to look and see that all joints are properly filled with mortar. Putting this repair off will only cost you more money later (like a collapsed wall!)

Chipped or peeling paint: Look around doors and windows to see if there is any chipping or peeling paint. If so, decide if you are going to cap over the windows or scrape and paint them. We recommend capping. We have never scraped and painted around windows and doors. The first time you cap them will be the last time you cap them. Scraping and painting will only last about 5 years and you'll be out there doing it again.

Porches: If your property has a porch, look up at the ceiling. If the paint is chipping and peeling, something has to be done and we have the perfect solution. Side it!

Once this is done, you'll never have to do it again.

House Number: Be sure your property has a house number on it. This is required by Section 8 so the mail can be delivered.

Enclosed Porches: Most enclosed porches have many windows. Sometimes anywhere upwards of 10 of them! This is a landlord's worst nightmare. For if all the windows are old, wood, inoperable, chipping, etc., they will all have to be replaced, right? Wrong! You only need 1 operable window per room, so just replace 1 window. The others, you will simply plywood and side over. A window costs about $120 and a piece of ½" plywood costs $20 and can cover over 2 windows. Not only that, once you eliminate a window, you have eliminated all chances of it ever getting broken. No baseballs smashing through it, no broken balancers or window locks, no problems, ever!

Six porch windows eliminated

Screen Door: If a screen door is opening and closing properly, we will leave it in place. If it is missing a chain, a handle, or closer, we would replace it before the tenant moves in. The first time a tenant calls us for a repair on it, or Section 8 fails us on an inspection for it, it's gone. We will remove it! You don't need a screen door to pass a Section 8 inspection.

Outside doors: Check to see if the door opens, closes and locks properly. If the key or latch is sticking and the lock is old, replace it. We have always used Kwikset deadbolts and door knobs. They are very easy to use, and we have found them to be very durable. Never use the double keyed lock, for they will not pass a Section 8 inspection.

The fear is that the tenant will remove the key from the inside lock and if there is a fire, they won't be able to get out.

Next, go inside the house and close the front door. If you see any daylight around the top, sides, or bottom of the door it will have to be corrected. The cheapest and easiest way to correct this problem is with weather stripping. Simply staple it to the top and side of the door. At the bottom of the door you will need to install a door sweep. They are also very easy to install.

If your front door is warped or must be replaced, replace it with a pre-hung steel door. The price of the pre-hung steel doors is about the same or a little cheaper than a solid wooden door. The benefit is that the door is already hinged for you. They go in rather easily and will last forever. A wooden door needs to be painted or stained whereas a steel door is fine with just its factory finish. Don't bother to ever paint it because once you paint it the first time, you will be painting it a second.

Another advantage of the steel door as opposed to the wooden door is that they come with the lock and doorknob holes already pre-drilled. On a solid core wooden door, you will need to purchase a hole saw bit and drill your own. The steel doors are a little cheaper, a lot quicker and last forever, making this a very easy choice. Choose steel!

Shrubbery: Be sure to eliminate all bushes, hedges, small trees, etc. from the front and rear of the property. A lot of times the tenant will not tend to them and they become overgrown. By eliminating them I mean cut them as far down as you can get them. Your home does not have to be well-landscaped to pass a Section 8 inspection. However, if the grass and trees are overgrown, you will fail an inspection somewhere down the line. Not only can you fail an inspection, but you may receive violations from the city for overgrown shrubbery. Eliminate the future problems by eliminating all your bushes, trees, hedges, etc.

These are all the things that you will be checking and looking for in the front of your property. If any of them need repairs, write them down and get ready to move onto your next step on the "checklist."

Inside the home: Now that the front of your home has been checked for repairs, we are going to go inside. We will be starting upstairs and working our way down to the basement. Always check the bedrooms first and start in the front or "master bedroom". This will be the next item on your checklist.

Master bedroom: The first thing you want to look at is the windows. Are they old, new, operable, wood, etc.? If they are the old wooden type, replace them and get it over with. You don't need the hassle of failing an inspection for a window with chipping paint, the window doesn't lock, the window won't stay up, etc. If you do your repairs right the first time after purchasing your property, it will make it so much easier every time after that! Don't be afraid to spend money on items such as windows because this is something that is going to be in the property for as long as you own it. It's the cosmetic things you want to eliminate spending on. I've seen landlords leave all the old windows in a house and then rip out and replace carpets that only needed cleaning. Gimme a break! In this business, carpets are only new the minute you put them down and may only last 5 years depending on the tenant. But if you put new windows in a home, I guarantee you will get 30 years out of them. I have never failed an inspection for having old carpet but have failed several for having a problem with a window. If you do already have vinyl windows, be sure that they lock and stay up on their own. Locks and balancers can be purchased at any hardware store and are easy to install.

Closets: You do **not** need a closet in a bedroom to pass inspection. The reason I am telling you this is because closets can become a real pain. It sometime seems as though the tenant wants to jam everything he or she owns into a very small closet. Not that this matters to you or me, but what happens is now the door won't close properly. Instead of taking some items out of the closet, the tenant proceeds to slam the door harder to get it closed. Instead of the door closing, you got it, it falls off its hinges. Now when the inspector comes out, he see's the door laying there and fails you. What can you do? One of two things. The first is to "seal off" the closet. Cover it with luan and/or plywood and paint over it. If the inspector never knew it was there, neither will the tenant and it will never become a problem.

The second solution is easier than the first! Remove the closet door before the tenant knocks it off. That's right, a closet doesn't need a door on it to pass inspection. It's that *preventive maintenance* we spoke of earlier. When making your checklists and you come to a closet, here is a good way to figure out what you should do:

1. If a closet door is in excellent condition and it is on hinges, leave it. The first time a tenant knocks it off its hinges, simply remove it.

2. If a closet door is in poor condition, doesn't close properly, hinges are loose, chipping and peeling paint, then you should remove the door before the tenant moves in.

3. Inspect inside the close. Look for broken shelves, missing or broken clothes rod, holes in the walls, chipping paint, etc. If these conditions exist, simply "seal off" the closet!

Floors: The next thing you're going to inspect is the floor. As you can probably tell by now, we're not very big fans of spending money on carpets, especially in bedrooms. If I am going to spend money on carpet, it's going to be in the living room and dining room. Like they say, "your first impression is a lasting impression" and if a tenant likes what he/she sees when they first open the door, they will most likely rent the house no matter what the bedroom floors look like. If the carpets that were on the floor when you purchased the house are in good or even fair condition, leave them. It's as simple as that!

If the carpets are worn, ripped, <u>very</u> stained or dry rotted, then something must be done. We have dedicated a whole section of this book to flooring. Every tip in the flooring section will save you thousands. When we first started out in this business it was in the flooring area where we made many costly mistakes. However, over time we corrected and perfected several ways to save time and money in this area. After reading our flooring section, you will know exactly what to write down on your checklist when you come to the floor of any room in the house!

<u>Bedroom doors:</u> The next thing you will be inspecting is the bedroom door. If your door is new or old, closes properly and locks, you're in good shape. Ninety percent of the time when purchasing old homes this is not the case. All bedrooms must have a properly working door that locks to pass a Section 8 inspection. Here are a few examples of what to do if this is not the case with your bedroom doors.

1. You have an old solid door that closes properly. The knob is old and doesn't have a lock on it. Do **not** remove the knob and install a new one. This will cost you about $8 and a ½ hour of man time. Simply buy a hook-n-eye (50 cents) and screw it on. This should take you two minutes and your bedroom door will pass inspection.

2. You have an old solid door that **doesn't** close or lock properly. Keep the door and change the knob. We always use Kwikset products because they are very durable and easy to install. Simply purchase a bedroom loor lock, install it, and your door will pass inspection.

3. You have an old solid door that is warped or broken beyond repair. It must be replaced. Simply measure your opening (most bedrooms will be 28" to 32" wide) and proceed to Home Depot to purchase your door. Do not, and I repeat, do not purchase a hollow core bedroom door. Although you may save yourself $20, these doors are not going to last the duration of one tenant. They may swing gracefully for 20 years in your residence or mine, but they ain't gonna do it in a rental. If your tenants are fighting between themselves and he/she locks themselves in a bedroom, it won't take much for the other to kungfo it down. Spend the extra $20 and go with a solid door. This way, maybe the $8 knob gives way, or the hinges pull out. You can always re-hinge a solid door. But I guarantee you this, unless your tenants name is Bruce Lee, he's not gonna splinter the door or punch a hole through it!

4. You have a new hollow door that is cracked or broken. Replace it with a solid door.

Bedroom: There's really not much to inspecting a bedroom. There's no water lines, only 1 switch, 1 light, and a couple of outlets. The other 4 things (windows, doors, closets and floors) are all very basic and common sense will tell you what you need to write down on your checklist while inspecting these items.

After completing your checklist in the master bedroom, move on to the next bedroom. Label this "bedroom #2", the next, "bedroom #3", and so on.

The things you inspected in the master bedroom are the same things you will be looking for in all the other bedrooms. By now your checklist should have several headings.

Bathrooms: The next room you will be inspecting is the bathroom. The first item you will inspect is the toilet. I'm going to give you 2 scenarios. Number one is if the water **is** lienable against the property you are renting out and you are paying the water bill for the property. Number two is if you are not paying the water bill and the water is **not** lienable. *Stop!* If you do not have any idea of what I am talking about right now then go the section entitled "Water Bills." It will explain to you how to find out if the water the tenant is using is leinable against your property. In some cities or states if a water bill is owed, the water company can put a lien on the property, so when you go to sell the property, it must get paid. Some water companies hold the tenant responsible for the water bill. Anyway, after you read the water bill section, you'll understand.

Scenario #1: Water is lienable, so you want to keep the water bills low. If your toilet is more than 20 years old, more than likely it is a 5 gallon toilet. Also, the parts inside it are 20 years old. REPLACE IT!

The toilet you are going to be replacing it with will be 1.5 or 1.6 gallon flush. This can be bought at Home Depot for around $48. We have been using them for 7 years now and don't have any complaints. Also, the money you save by flushing 1.6 gallons of water as opposed to 5 gallons of water each flush will pay for the toilet itself in about 6 months.

Scenario #2: Water is not lienable, the water bill is in the tenant's name. It will not matter to you how high the water bill is. If your toilet is old, you can leave it. It's probably not a bad idea to install a flush kit.

They consist of a Fluidmaster, flapper valve, and toilet handle. They are all easy to install and will give your toilet added life.

Also, when replacing a toilet, we always use a Johnny wax ring. They are a little thicker than a regular wax ring and do a better job of preventing leaks from around the base of the toilet. They only cost about a dollar more than a regular wax ring but consider it a dollar well spent.

Tub: The next item in the bathroom you will be inspecting is the tub. There are four things in the tub area you will be looking for. The first and most expensive is the faucet. Simply check the tub spout to see if it is leaking. Turn the water off and on. If there are no drips, you're good – leave it alone. If the water doesn't stop dripping, there's a problem.

Most of your old homes have what's called a three handle tub diverter.

No matter what the make of your diverter, all can easily be re-washered and re-seated. This should stop your leak. If not, your next step would be to replace your stems. The easiest way to get the right one is to take one with you to your plumbing supply store. Tell them you need a hot, cold, and a shower diverter stem. Also, tell them you need new seats. Never replace a stem without installing a new seat. What you're trying to do is save yourself the time and money it would take to install a completely new tub diverter. Ninety-five percent of the time, changing washers, seats and stems will take care of your problem. Now, I'll get to that other 5%.

You did everything you could do and your tub still leaks. You must change your tub faucet. Even though you have a 3-valve tub diverter on your tub now, this is not what you will be replacing it with. **Never** purchase a 3-handle tub diverter. Why? Because there are three stems that can leak, three washers that can go bad, three o-rings that can leak and 3 seats that can rot. If you're going to be sweating on a new diverter, make it a Moen single-handle diverter.

They cost about the same, but you get way less headaches from them. If you're single-handle diverter leaks, simply pull out the cartridge and replace it with a new one. You're done! NO more leak!

Showerhead: The next item in the tub area you will inspect is the shower head. Simply turn on the shower. If water flows freely through the head, leave it. If water flows freely through the head but leaks from the threads, remove the showerhead, add some Teflon tape and screw the head back on. This will take care of your problem. If water is not flowing freely through your showerhead, install a new one. They're cheap and easy to install.

Caulk: **Always recaulk your tub!** Start by using a razor knife or scraper to remove all your old caulk. Put a nice thin bead into the cracks and then finger the caulk in. This will prevent any leaks and give your tub a neat, clean appearance.

Shower curtain rod: All Section 8 properties require a shower curtain rod to pass inspection. You want to also install a $5 shower curtain although the curtain is not required by Section 8. Just because you put a shower rod up does not guarantee your tenant will cooperate and install a shower curtain. Believe me, I've seen it happen more than once. Two weeks after a tenant moves in, they call you for a leak coming through their dining room ceiling. You proceed upstairs to see where the water is coming from. Whatta ya know? Your new tenant never put up a shower curtain. Now you possibly have a damaged bathroom floor and definitely a damaged dining room ceiling. Spend the extra five bucks on a curtain and avoid this call. You are now finished inspecting the tub area.

Bathroom sink: The next item in the bathroom you will be inspecting is the bathroom sink. If you have a wall-mounted sink, remove it and replace it with a vanity.

Over the years we have found that the wall-mounted basins sometimes get ripped from the wall. Also, the trap is exposed with no protection surrounding it. A vanity will eliminate both of these future repairs. The faucet we use is also a single-handled Moen. The same holds true for a Moen basin faucet. If it leaks simply replace the cartridge.

The next item in the bathroom you will be inspecting is the window. As we mentioned in the beginning of this section, if it is wood, replace it. When renting a property with Section 8, you must have some type of ventilation in your bathroom to pass inspection. Ventilation can be in any of these 3 forms: a window, a skylight, or an exhaust fan.

If you do not have a window or a skylight you will be using option 3, an exhaust fan. If you don't have a window, chances are there is a skylight available. Make sure your skylight opens and closes freely. If not, some oil or WD-40 on the wheel should do the trick. If it still won't open, you or your roofer should check outside the skylight to be sure it's not mucked shut with roofing tar. If your skylight is beyond repair, you can have any roofer install a new one. A new skylight should cost you between $200 and $250 depending on the roofer.

Floor: The next item in the bathroom you will be inspecting is the floor. If it is ceramic, leave it alone.

You're already in good shape. You don't have to worry about water popping up any tiles and failing you on inspection day. I've seen landlords put stick down tiles over a perfectly good ceramic floor because they didn't like the color of it. What a waste of money! You're not trying to win a beauty contest here, you're trying to rent a house. And besides, now you have the chance of the stick down tiles getting wet and popping up. Leave the ceramic floor alone!

If you have stick down tiles or a one-piece vinyl floor that is in need of replacement, go to our 'Flooring' section. This will give you a good idea on what decision you should make.

Bathroom door: The final item you will be inspecting in the bathroom is the door. Be sure that it closes properly and locks. If it needs to be replaced, use a solid core door.

Hallway and Steps: There's not very much to inspect in this area. You have no doors, windows, water lines, etc. so this area of your inspection should go rather quickly. The only thing you need in your upstairs hallway to pass inspection is a smoke detector. Place it on the ceiling at the top of the steps and you're done. Next, move onto the staircase. If you have carpet on the steps, inspect each step for loose carpet or tripping hazards. If any are found, simply use a staple gun to tighten them back up. If there are no carpets, check each tread for cracks. If cracks are found, you must replace that tread. The next item you need to look at is the railing. If one exists, be sure that it is tight and secure. All Section 8 properties must have a railing if the height of the steps exceeds 36 inches. If your staircase is missing a railing, one must be installed.

The last thing you need to check in the staircase area are the spindles. If your staircase has spindles and 1 or more are missing, they must be replaced. A Section 8 inspector will fail you if one is missing. The fear here is that a young child could fall between the spindles if they are too far apart. Remember, you are providing safe and decent housing.

The living room and dining room: You're are now ready to move into the living room and dining room area. We call these rooms "the money rooms." These are the first rooms your tenant will see when they open the door. I'm not telling you to put down $25 per yard carpet and wallpaper the joint, I'm just saying make sure these two rooms look bright and clean. It will make it much easier to rent the house.

Living Room: Let's get back to what to look for on your living room check list. The first thing you want to look at is the windows. You need at least one window to pass inspection. Most rowhome living rooms have two windows. If they are wood, replace them. If they are vinyl, make sure they lock and stay up on their own. The same rules apply to your dining room window or windows. At the bottom of the steps in the living room, you will need to install a smoke detector on the ceiling. If one or both of these rooms has a closet, apply the same rules and information we spoke of while inspecting a bedroom closet. Your main goal in the living room and dining room is to be sure these rooms look good. Don't be afraid to spend a couple extra bucks on mini-blinds in these two rooms. It might pay off!

Kitchen: Now we will be moving to the kitchen. There are several things you will need in your kitchen to pass a Section 8 inspection. The first thing is ventilation. If there is a window in the kitchen, this should be sufficient. If you do not have a window in the kitchen, you will need to install an exhaust fan over the stove.

Simply measure your stove (it will be 30" or 36") and purchase your fan at any electrical supply house or at Home Depot. The exhaust fan must be installed at least 30" above the stove. Once you're done getting your ventilation in place, move on to the stove. All Section 8 properties require you provide the tenant with a working stove.

Inspecting a Stove:

1. Always replace your gas line and install a gas cock or shut off valve. By changing these two things, you can just about eliminate getting a call from a tenant saying they smell gas leaking from the stove. The only smell of gas they can get is if their pilot is out. Tell them to simply light the pilot and have a nice day!

2. Inspecting the burners: The first thing your inspector will do when checking the stove is turn on all four burners. All four had better come on or you just failed the inspection. If your pilot is lit and the burner is <u>not</u> coming on, one or several of

the gas portholes are clogged. Take a paper clip and stick it through each hole on the burner. Ninety-nine percent of the time this should do the trick.

3. Inspecting the oven: If your oven is self-igniting, turn it up to 400°. If your oven doesn't have a self-ignitor, light it and turn it up to 400°. Come back in five minutes. If it's hot, you're good. If it's not, you have a bad thermostat. Call an appliance repair man out to your property and have him install a thermostat will probably cost about $150. If your stove is newer and in good condition, that would be the right move. If your stove is older and not in good condition, replace it!

4. Replacing your stove: For years we have been replacing our old stoves with a Tappan.

These stoves can be purchased at Best Buy for $245. Considering you would be paying $150 for just a thermostat this is quite a bargain. And, although the stoves are rather cheap in cost, we have never had a problem or complaint about them. If you cannot find a place that carries these stoves, try to find something similar in value. One thing you want to steer clear of when purchasing a new stove is electronic ignitors. All four burners have one and they go bad quite often and are very expensive to repair. Stick with the old-fashioned pilots. If they go out, relight them with a match rather than spending $80 for a repairman to fix a wire. A match is much cheaper!

Refrigerator: The other appliance in the kitchen you will be checking is the refrigerator. You'll be checking to make sure you don't have one. You don't need a refrigerator to pass a Section 8 inspection so why provide one? It only gives you an extra reason to fail an inspection or receive a tenant's complaining phone call. Have the tenant provide his/her own refrigerator. They will also have to sign a Section 8 form saying they will always have a working refrigerator in their home.

Kitchen Faucet: The next items in the kitchen you will be inspecting is the sink and faucet. Check them both for leaks. If your faucet is leaking and appears to be old, replace it. The faucet to replace it with, once again, is the single-lever Moen. I know I keep mentioning these faucets but, again, I must express to you how much we believe in these Moen products. I've been in this field for a fairly long time now and have used many other products, but I have found none more durable or simpler to repair than a Moen faucet. When purchasing your Moen kitchen sink faucet, be sure not to buy one with a sprayer. They cost a little more and add one more thing that can possibly break. There's two things you don't need, spending more money and a problem to boot.

Kitchen Sink: Next comes the sink. Run the water and see if you have a leak. If you do, put in your sink stopper and let the sink fill up about halfway. Let the water stand for a minute and if you don't see the water leaking from underneath, it's not your sink that's leaking – it's the trap. If once the sink is filled and is leaking from underneath of the sink, you should be able to find the hole. Don't bother trying the plug the hole with bondo or clogging it with plumbers' putty. It will only come back to haunt you down the line. Replace the sink and be done with it. The sink we use is an inexpensive stainless steel sink. You should get at least 15 years out of any stainless steel sink no matter what type of abuse your tenant puts it through.

If water is leaking from the trap, it could be a bad washer or a hole in the trap. Go to our 'Plumbing" section. It will tell you what type of washer, trap, gauge of trap, etc. to use and when to use it. Also, when inspecting the trap, be sure to see if your sink has a garbage disposal.

Garbage disposal: If your property has a garbage disposal, eliminate it immediately. I don't care if it's brand new, working great and cost $150! Get rid of it! Unless you like headaches and that's exactly what they are. Your tenant will call you at least 5 times per year for garbage disposal problems. They clog up your sink, the blades get stuck, the reset button pops off, you name it, it happens. And you'll never get an *honest* answer from your tenants when you ask them what they threw down the sink. However, you will get the *same* answer, "Nothing! I didn't throw nothing down it!" When you start pulling chicken bones and plastic forks out of the garbage disposal your tenants turn into confused actors. A surprised look will come across their face when they tell you "I don't know how that got down there." I do! Instead of scraping their plates into the trash can, they now scrape them into the sink. Eliminate problems before they become problems and, believe me, a garbage disposal will become more than one problem.

Cabinets: Let me just touch on this subject very briefly. If your cabinets are old but working properly, leave them. Remember, this isn't where you live and none of your friends will be coming over to enjoy a 7-course meal at your rental property. If the cabinets are working properly but are a real eyesore, paint them. A gallon or two of paint is much cheaper than rehabbing your entire kitchen. Even if some cabinets are off the hinges or missing hardware, all of these things can be repaired rather quickly and inexpensively. Bottom line – do whatever you can to save the cabinets that are there. Your last resort would be to replace them.

Countertops: Most of the time your countertops size is adequate, providing enough space to prepare food. In some situations, it is not. In order to pass a Section 8 inspection, you need at least 4 linear feet of food prep space. If we don't have enough space we simply cut a countertop to 4' and attach it to the wall. Strap a 2" × 4" across the back wall, sit your countertop on top of it and make 2 legs out of 2" × 4"'s. Problem solved.

Kitchen Floor: The last item in the kitchen you will be inspecting is the floor. Once again, if it is ceramic, leave it. You can never go wrong with a ceramic floor. If your floor is stick down tiles or a one-piece linoleum and they are in good condition, they can also be left alone. The only time I recommend changing a floor is if it is going to fail you on an inspection. That would be if the floor is missing tiles, the ceramic floor is cracked, or your linoleum is ripped. For more on when, how to and why to change a floor, go to our 'Flooring' section.

Basement Door: The next room you will be moving onto is the basement steps and hallway. The first thing you will inspect is the basement door. All Section 8 inspections require a door here. All doors leading to the basement must have a lock in order to prevent children from entering the basement. A bedroom door knob lock or a hook-n-eye will do. Once again, if your door needs replacement, replace it with a solid core door. The next thing you will need to pass inspection is a railing from the top basement step to the bottom step. If you have an all cement basement, you will have to attach the railing to the steps instead of to the party wall.

Basement Steps: If your basement steps are concrete, you have nothing to do. If they are wood, check to see that all the treads are okay. If any are cracked, simply cover over them with a new tread. We always paint our basements steps gray because it gives the basement a clean appearance when first entering. The next thing you want to do is make sure your steps have braces under them. If not, add them. Some of the things your tenants will be bringing down the basement steps are going to be quite heavy and may collapse your staircase if it is not braced properly.

Finally, you will be adding a smoke detector at the bottom of the steps. Now it's time to move down to the basement!

Basement: Although this is the room your tenants will be spending the least amount of time in, it more than likely is the room you will spend the most amount of time in when rehabbing your property. There are so many repairs and future repairs that you can eliminate in the basement. You may have to spend a little more time down here, but it will be worth it if you don't have to come back.

The first thing in the basement you want to write on your checklist is what to eliminate. The answer is everything. Everything that does not serve a purpose, that is! Paneling, old work benches, closets, carpets, partitions, washers, dryers, etc. Bring it down to the bare walls.

Like we've been saying all along, the less that's there, the less to repair. Once you are down to the bare walls, you can now look at them and see what kind of condition they are in. If your walls are all solid concrete, lucky you! You don't have to do anything, and you will pass inspection. Most of the time in old houses this is not the case. The walls are usually made of dirt, clay and plaster. When the plaster covering the walls gets old, it starts to deteriorate. The dirt or clay behind the plaster falls to the floor and your property fails inspection.

You now have to repair the walls. Here is where we will save you a ton of money and a ton of time! Ninety-nine percent of the investors in this business would use sand, lime and cement to repair the basement walls. Not us! Buying and mixing sand, lime and cement is expensive and time consuming. If you mix it too dry, you lose half of it in the cement pan. If you mix it too wet, it falls off the wall. You just can't win. Use the product we use and you will be a winner every time. By now I'm sure you're on the edge of your seat wondering what the hell do these guys use that is cheaper and just as strong as sand, lime and cement. But I gotta play with ya a little more. Not only is it cheaper and just as durable, it sticks to the wall better, mixes faster and covers more area. The product is called StructoLite, and boy does it work!

It comes in 50 lb. bags and mixes with just water. You mix it to a peanut buttery consistence, slap it on the walls, and you're done. The stuff dries as hard as iron. You can purchase it at Home Depot and it's worth every penny.

Water heater: Now that your basement walls are ready for inspection, let's get to the next item the inspector will be checking. The water heater! What he will be looking for is a blow off tube. A blow off tube is simply an extension of the pressure relief valve which must extend down to within 8" of the floor.

Your blow off tube does not have to be made of copper, PVC will do. The inspector will also check your breaker box. If you have fuses, be sure all the fuses are there. If you are missing any fuses, you will fail the inspection. Simply screw in fuses where needed. If you are missing a breaker, close off the open hole with a breaker box blank. The fear here is that a child will stick his finger in an open hole on your service panel. Inspect all of your junction boxes to be sure they have covers on them. No cover, no pass. Also be sure that your wires are not fraying or covered with electrical tape. We have dedicated an entire section on 'Electrical'. It will tell you everything in the home to inspect, eliminate, and replace. It will tell you the exact products we use.

The next thing you want to inspect are the pipes in the ceiling. Not your copper pipes but your heating pipes. A lot of times in these old houses, the pipes have been painted. If yours have been, make sure the paint is not chipping or peeling. If they are, scrape them and paint them. We always use black Rustoleum. Black because it hides the dirt and Rustoleum because it lasts. It may cost a little more, but it covers in one coat and holds up for years.

Ventilation: The next items you want to check are the basement windows. Every basement must have a least one window for ventilation in order to pass Section 8 inspection. If you have two or more, this is also fine. Be sure that all your windows lock. If your windows are old and need to be replaced, do **not** replace more than one. You only need one to pass inspection so one is all you will be replacing. The others you will be sealing off. Here's why. I don't know what it is about basement windows, but tenants love to break 'em, and once they're broken, they never want to take responsibility for it. When a tenant locks themselves out, they don't want to pay a lockout fee or kick their door down. So what happens? Their foot goes right through the basement window. They unlock it, let themselves in and are quick to call you and tell you to get over to their house because somebody (usually a kid out front playing ball) broke their basement window. Since the basement window is street level, they think you'll buy their story. First of all, our lease has a window waiver saying we are not responsible for any broken windows no matter who did it. But you're still going to get the bullshit story and an argument. Eliminate the story and the argument. When installing your new basement window, only replace the back basement window. Eliminate the front by sealing it off with plywood and siding.

Ninety-nine percent of the activity is going on in front of the house, not the back. Your front window stands a 100% chance of not getting broken because it's not there anymore. If the back window gets broken, it would have to have been done by somebody in the yard. And who's the only one that's supposed to be in the yard? That's right, your tenants.

The basement window we use is called a hopper window and can be purchased at Home Depot for about $40. That's about 1/3 of the cost of getting a window made for the exact size of your opening. The hoppers are smaller than a regular sized window and the smaller the window, the smaller the chances of it getting broken.

Basement door: The final item in the basement to inspect will be the basement door (if your property has one). All Section 8 properties need at least 2 doorways from which you can exit and enter the home. Be sure your basement door has a lock, closes properly, and is weather proof. Weather stripping and a door sweep may have to be used if you can see daylight on the sides or at the bottom of the basement door. This will complete your interior inspection.

The final item you will be inspecting is the rear or back of the property. The first thing you want to look at is the brick pointing. The same rules apply to pointing in the rear of the house as do in the front of the house as well as the guidelines for shrubbery removal.

Next look at your service wire (electrical wire).

Be sure that it is not fraying or that the plastic jacket covering it is not split. If it is, you will fail your inspection. It must be replaced. In our 'Electrical' section, we explain and go over the cost of this repair.

Next, look at the outside of your rear windows and decide if they need to be capped. The typical price to cap a window is about $40. That's what we pay. If you own a couple of properties and need a lot of windows capped, you may be able to work out a better deal in volume. Also check your bargeboard at the top of the property. If this is in poor condition, also have it capped. We pay $75 per board.

If your property has rear steps, be sure they are not cracking or chipping. Also, if they are over 36" high, you will need a railing.

This will now complete your checklist. Let's start crossing it off.

CHAPTER 8

WATER BILLS

THE BEST TIPS EVER ON KEEPING THEM DOWN

First things first, let's make sure this chapter applies to you. If you're lucky, it won't. The first thing that you have to find out is if the water bill is *lienable*. What this means is if the water bill is placed in the tenant's name and they don't pay it, the water company can attach a lien to the property. Now, when you go to sell your property, the money that is owed to the water company will come directly out of your proceeds. It doesn't matter whose name the bill was in because the lien is placed against the property. In Philadelphia, the water bill is lienable. In the suburbs just outside of Philadelphia, it is not lienable. It all depends on where your home is located.

To figure out if your water bill is lienable all you have to do is call the water company on your bill. Ask them if the water is lienable or not lienable. If it is not, you're in good shape. Your tenant can run the bill up to say $1,000, move out of the property, never pay it, and nothing will ever come back to haunt you. If this is the boat you're in, skip to the next section. You won't need any of these tips.

Now for all you unlucky folks who are still with me, let's get started. First, since the water is lienable, I keep the bill in my name even if the tenant is responsible for the water usage. I want the bill to come directly to me, so I know it's getting paid. Once I receive it, I will make a copy of it and send it out to my tenant. In turn, they send me a money order for the amount due. I treat the water just as I do the rent. Late fees apply, and if I don't get a money order from the tenant within 15 days after sending out a bill, I start an eviction. If they don't pay in 15 days your probably aren't ever getting paid. Nothing is different, money is money. It doesn't matter if you're getting beat for $700 rent or a $40 water bill. If you're getting beat, you've got to do something about it.

One thing you can do about it is help the tenant keep the water bill low. If the bill is only $35 as opposed to $100 you are more likely to get paid. Do you know how a water bill gets up to $100? It's called waste or abuse. Take your pick as to what sounds nicer, but they are both one in the same. What can you do to 'help' your tenant avoid high water bills? The answer is a lot!

First, let me tell you some stories/nightmares of tenants abusing water. All of these stories in one way or another helped us come up with different strategies in preventing high water bills. Strategies that I believe are the best in the business!

Now, when we first started out in this business, here is how we set up our leases. For a three bedroom property, we would receive $700 per month. We would leave the tenant responsible for the water bill. Once the water bill came in, we would send a copy of it out to the tenant and tell them that they had 10 days to pay it. What a nightmare. You would hear every excuse in the book, or you wouldn't hear from them at all. Since a water bill is usually only $35 to $40 a month, the tenants would act as though you couldn't evict them over so low an amount.

One woman had the nerve to say to me, "I can't believe you're coming around here knocking on my door for $33."

My response to her was, "If I owed you $33 you would be camped out on my front lawn!"

Anyway, it got to be such a pain in the ass that something had to be changed. We called Section 8, told them how much of a problem we were having collecting the water bills, and asked them to come up with some type of solution or we were pulling the plug. We would not be renewing any leases once they expired. What we were told nearly blew us away. You see, not only do the tenants get their rent paid by Section 8, but every month they also receive a utility check. So all along, the tenants were receiving the money for the water from Section 8, but they were not sending it to us.

The solution we and Section 8 came up with was simple. Once again, the rent being paid to us for a person with a 3 bedroom voucher was $700. The tenant was responsible for the water bill. The amount the tenant was given for water in their utility check was $48. What we did was have Section 8 bring the rent amount up to $748 while the tenant would be getting $48 less in their utility check. In about 98% of the cases, this solution worked out fine. Most tenants kept their water

ie. decreased utility check to tenant
increased rent direct to landlord

bills below $48, so they either broke even or made a couple of bucks. In the other 2% of the cases, it didn't work out so well.

Ya see, once the tenant found out that the landlord was now paying the water, all hell broke out. In July of 2001, we received a water bill from one of our properties for $418. Immediately, we called the tenant and said we were only paying $48 worth of the water bill and she would be responsible for paying the rest. Of course, the first words out of her mouth were, "My water bill is included in with the rent, I don't have to pay no water bill!" Other tenants who normally would have a $44 water bill when they were responsible for it now began to get bills of $90 to $100. Sometimes even more. Now we had to come up with another solution.

I'm telling you, sometimes you think you're at war in this business. You gotta fight fire with fire. If you don't think at least two steps ahead of these people, you will get burned. What we did was draw up a form for our tenants to sign. Here is what it looks like.

NEW TENANT
Water Bill Excess Usage Form

The allotted usage and service charge for a 3 bedroom unit is $48. Should you go over your allotted amount, you will be charged accordingly.

The allotted usage and service charge for a 2 bedroom unit is $37. Should you go over your allotted amount, you will be charged accordingly.

By signing below, you are agreeing to the above terms.

Landlord Signature   Tenant Signature

This form was placed in our lease. If the tenant was already in the property, we put it in as an addendum to the lease. Basically, what it says is, if Section 8 was only giving you $48 worth of water in your utility check, then that's all we are giving you. Anything over $48, the tenant will be responsible. I don't care if they went $5 over the amount, they are paying it. If you own 300 homes and everyone goes over the amount by $5, that's $1,500 you're out.

Now, let me get you back to the story of the lady with the $418 water bill. After telling Nick and I that she was not responsible for the water bill, we told her to check her lease. After reading the part that said she was responsible for over usage, the excuses started. "I have a leak somewhere in this house," she said.

"I don't care. Read a little bit further into your lease and you'll see that we are not responsible for leaks either," Nick replied back.

Of course, the next thing she told us was we had better get out to her property and find the leak because when she gets a high water bill next month, she won't be paying that one either. I love when a tenant gives you such empty threats. It's really cut and dry in this business. If you pay, you stay; no dough, you go! It's even easier when you have a lease that they signed which says the same thing. Anyway, Nick and I went out to her property the next day to check for a leak. The first thing we did was put our ear to the vent out front.

If water is leaking or running in the property, you will hear it at the vent. We didn't hear a thing. We knocked on the door and the woman let us in. We started in the bathroom and found no leaks, went down the basement and found no leaks. Last, but not least, was the kitchen. Again, no leaks. One thing Nick noticed was the whole time we were checking for the "phantom leak" the woman stood in front of the back door. Just before we were about to leave, Nick asked her to move out of the way so he could check out back.

"Everything is fine out back," she promised. Nick walked into the dining room and looked out back into the yard. Whatta ya know! The woman had a rubber pool as big as the yard. No filter on it, she would just dump it when it got dirty and fill it up the next day. Why not? She thought Uncle Mike and Uncle Nick were paying for it. That was the last pool that anybody filled up in our backyard. What did we do? Eliminated the rear hose bib! Here's what to do:

#1. Turn off your water main in the house.

#2. Trace as far back to where your copper for your hose bib begins.

#3. Using a pipe cutter, cut the copper line.

#4. Solder a ½" cap onto the open line.

#5. Remove the hose bib hook-up.

#6. Plug the hole where the hose bib was with caulk or cement.

#7. Turn water main back on.

For the price of a 10 cent copper cap, you just eliminated somebody filling a pool in your yard. Besides, why do they need a hose out back? It's not like they're going to be watering your grass!

Water bill nightmare #2 began when Nick and I received a water bill from a tenant for $386. First thing we do is pick up the phone and call the tenant to tell her she owes $338 ($386 - $48 = $338) Well, there's another utility she's not keeping up with and that's her phone – it's disconnected. We get in the truck and drive over to the property with bill in hand. Before we even get out of the truck we figured out what the problem was. The tenant was running a full-service car wash right in front of our house! You guessed it, bye bye front hose bibs.

Another thing that happens if you leave your front and rear hose bibs is that they freeze and burst in the wintertime. Never do the tenants turn them off from inside the home. Now you're risking water running out front and freezing on the sidewalk. What comes next? A lawsuit! Somebody will fall or at least claim that they fell on your property and you will have a lawsuit on your hands. It's so much easier to cut and cap the lines and be done with it. Once again, my favorite slogan applies here, "You don't need a hose bib to pass a Section 8 inspection, so why have one?"

Water bill nightmare #3 occurred when we, once again, received another high water bill, $404 to be exact. I called the tenant and asked, "Mrs. Green, what's going on over there?"

"Nothing is leaking, your water bill must be wrong."

Now, I hate hearing that because I know my water bill is not wrong. How do I know it's not wrong? Because the minute we purchase a home, we check to see that it has an automatic meter. If it does not have an automatic meter, we have the water company come out and install one. I don't know about your city, but in the City of Philadelphia, there is no charge to install an automatic meter. What it does is gives you an exact reading of how much water went through the meter. With the old meters, if the water company couldn't get into your home they would *estimate* your bill. Now, it's exactly correct every time. Since Mrs. Green is already giving me excuses, I know she is covering something up. It's time to put on my Sherlock Holmes hat and trench coat and go investigate again. What am I going to find this time? Another pool? Carwash? Has my tenant opened up the world's largest aquarium? No – how about a laundromat! That's exactly what she was running.

When we went to investigate the leak, the minute we hit the basement we knew what was up. One side of the basement looked like a Goodwill drop off location. Dirty laundry was piled up about 3 feet high. On the other side of the basement, laundry was neatly cleaned and folded and placed in boxes which had different names written on them. When I called the tenant down to the basement and asked her if she was running a laundromat, her answer was, "No, I just do wash for people who don't have washer machines. They give me a little bit of money for my trouble." Uh, yeah, I think that's called a laundromat! I told her to shut it down and pay the excess usage charge or I would evict her. What I really should have done was thank her! Why? Because in our fit of rage we came up with a great idea. We came up with an idea that will save you at least a third on your water bills. From here on out we started eliminating the washer and dryer hook-ups. No tenant could move into one of our properties until the washer and dryer hook-ups were cut and capped off.

If a tenant is moving into our property, they had better be prepared to visit the real laundromat once or twice per week. There's also three more *bonus benefits* you receive when you eliminate the washer and dryer hook-ups. The first is electric calls. You wouldn't believe the age and size of some of the washers and dryers these people want to hook up in your property. I often wonder what came first, the washboards or their washer.

Old washboard   *Actual tenant's washer*

These old washers and dryers blow fuses and trip breakers like there's no tomorrow. By eliminating the hook-ups, you also eliminate the future electric calls that would have come along with them.

The second bonus you receive is you eliminate a fire hazard. Once these washers and dryers get to a certain age, they also become a fire hazard. Wires melt together, motors burn up, etc. Another fire hazard that occurs is lint fires. Most of the time the tenant will not install (or will not properly install) a dryer vent. Now your basement rafters, ceiling and walls become covered in lint. One spark, and your property goes up in smoke. Eliminate your hook-ups, eliminate future fire hazards.

The third bonus has to do with inspections. Passing or failing to be exact. Remember when I told you about the enormous size of some of the washers going down your basement steps? Well let me tell you what happens when the washer does not fit down the steps. The railing that you spent time and money on to pass the inspection gets ripped down and thrown in the corner. Now the washer and dryer can fit down the steps. When your property gets inspected a year later, the railing is still laying in the corner. You need a railing to pass inspection and if yours is laying in the corner, you just failed. Eliminate your hook-ups, eliminate future failed inspections.

Now let me walk you through step by step how to eliminate your washer and dryer hook-up.

WASHER: #1. Turn off water main.
            #2. Trace your hot and cold washer water lines as far
               back as possible.
            #3. Cut them with pipe cutter.

#4. Solder a ½" cap to open lines and you're done with the washer.

DRYER: #1. Turn off gas main at meter.

#2. Eliminate gas line back to the Tee.

#3. Depending on size of gas line, plug threaded opening with a ½" cap or ½" plug. Always be sure to use pipe dope. You're finished with the dryer hook-up.

A 1½" rubber cap can be purchased at any plumbing supply or Home Depot for about $1.50. By eliminating these three things, front hose bib, rear hose bib, and washer/dryer hook-ups, you are guaranteeing yourself that your tenant will not be wasting or abusing the water in these three areas. Now there are other areas in your home where you have no choice but to give your tenants running water, such as the kitchen sink, bathroom sink, tub and toilet, but there are also ways to lower the water bill in these areas.

Starting with the toilet. I also mentioned several of these things in the "writing your checklist" section of the book but some of you perhaps only purchased the book for water bill saving tips, so I'll mention them again. If you have a 5 gallon toilet and you are paying the water bill, get rid of it! Replace it with a new 1.6 gallon flush toilet. The money you save within the first 6 months of installing the toilet will pay for itself.

Kitchen and bathroom faucets should have aerators. Aerators will increase your water pressure while using less water. Also, be sure that your aerators are cleaned out so as much water will flow through them as possible. Sometimes dirt and carbides get clogged in the aerator which decreases the water pressure.

Showerheads should be replaced with water saving showerheads. This head increases your water pressure and also uses less water. They can be purchased at any plumbing supply or Home Depot.

Believe me, if you do each and everything in this section before your tenant moves in, you will save at least 60% on your water bills. Rarely do I have a tenant go over on the water usage and if he/she does, I have three or four less places to check for leaks. Don't get lazy and eliminate 1 or 3 things, eliminate all of them. Don't start feeling sorry for anybody by thinking, "Gee, I wouldn't like to live without a washer or a hose." Otherwise, you're going to start feeling sorry for yourself when the water bill rolls in.

Keeping the water bill low is like a game of war. You have to try and think a step ahead of your enemy (which, in this case, would be the tenants). You have to try and eliminate anything they can use to destroy you (which would be hose bibs and washers). If you forget or neglect one small item, you risk a chance of losing the war. It's like an old saying my dad always says, "For the want of a nail, a war was lost." Here's how it goes:

A LITTLE NEGLECT MAY BREED MISCHIEF
by Ben Franklin

For the want of a nail the shoe was lost, for want of a shoe the horse was lost, for want of a horse the rider was lost, being overtaken and slain by the enemy, all for the want of care about a horse shoe nail.

Now, I don't know what Ben Franklin or my Dad got out of this quote, but here's my take on it. Some lazy blacksmith back in 1776 only put five nails into a horseshoe instead of six which were needed. He thought, "Ahh, that's good enough," as he slapped the horse on his ass and sent the rider on his way. The horseshoe ended up falling off and everything went downhill from there.

Don't be the lazy landlord who eliminates 5 out of 6 things that need to be eliminated because chances are that one thing that you did not eliminate will be the one that ends up costing you.

My final thought on keeping the water bills down is: verbal warnings and acting on them works! If your tenant is $1 over his or her allotted usage, speak up, let them know about it. Tell them you're not the type of landlord who turns their head the other way when it comes to water abuse. If every other tenant can keep their bill under $48, then so can they! I can think of 100 better things I can do with a dollar besides paying *somebody else's* water bill. Once you have already left, let's say, a washer hook-up in the property, it's going to be 10 times harder to eliminate it once you've moved your tenant in. Now they think it belongs there and that they deserve it. Had you eliminated it before they moved in, they would have never abused it or even known that it existed. Eliminate EVERYTHING and win the war on water bills. Whoever said winnng isn't everything, probably never had to pay a $386 dollar water bill.

CHAPTER 9

FLOORING AND CEILINGS

I'll get right to the point. I hate spending money on new carpets! I can't think of a bigger waste of money than spending money to install carpets in a rental property. Sometimes the carpets don't last more than 5 years. It's not that we were putting down cheap carpet which was as thin as Christmas wrapping paper either. The stuff we were installing was 20 year carpet at $10 per yard. It might have lasted 20 years in my house or yours, but you would be lucky to get 10 years out of it in theirs. I'll give you a David Letterman top 10 reasons why I hate installing carpeting:

#10. Mom, I spilled my glass of Hawaiian Punch all over the living room carpet. "Don't worry about it, baby, it's the landlord's carpet."

#9. Do you really think the no eating or drinking in the living room rule is going to be enforced?

#8. The "Please Remove Your Shoes" sign ain't gonna work either!

#7. How often do you think they will have the Chem-Dry guy over the house for a cleaning? Let me give you a hint – What comes before number one?

#6. God forbid, they sneak a pet into your property. You can evict the tenant, but you won't be evicting the fleas or the cat piss smell anytime soon.

#5. Half the people you're renting to don't own a vacuum.

#4. *You* won't be laying on it or running your toes through it, but *you* will be replacing it.

#3. There's cheaper and better ways to make a floor look good, and stay looking good.

#2. It's too expensive of an investment for possibly only a 3 year return.

AND THE #1 REASON WHY I HATE INSTALLING CARPETS IS: You don't need carpets to pass an inspection!

I will only replace the carpet in a house or room if it is the last resort. If water has buckled the floor boards or the flooring under the carpet looks like a jig-saw puzzle, then you have no other choice. Now let me tell you about a couple of ways of getting around replacing carpets.

#1. Leave what you have down. If the carpets were good enough for the people who were living in the home, then they're good enough for your tenant. Who cares if they look like they're right out of the 1970s. As long as they don't have holes in them and are not fraying, clean 'em and call it a day!

#2. You purchase the house and decide that the carpets are destroyed beyond cleaning or repair. Stained, ripped, pet odor, the whole nine yards! This does not necessarily mean you will be replacing the carpets. Once you remove the destroyed carpets, take a look at what's under them. If it's a rowhome, about 99% of the time it's hardwood flooring. About 80% of the time the hard woods are in good or excellent shape. If you can get away with mopping them and throwing some hardwood floor wax on them, great. If they look like they are pretty hammered with scratches and fading, have them restored. It's still cheaper than carpet. Our guy will come out to the home, sand and varnish every room in the house for $600 (3 bedroom house, add $100 for each additional bedroom). So what if they don't take their shoes off, so what if they spill soda on the floor, so what if they eat in the living room. A spill isn't going to ruin hardwoods. That's what's great about them. They may not look as nice as carpet or be as comfortable, but unless you plan to spend the night over your tenant's house, who cares what they're walking on.

Here's another thing to chew on. Carpets can fail you on an inspection. Hardwoods never will! Loose carpet can create a tripping hazard, but if there is no carpet there, there won't be any tripping hazards.

Let's imagine that you need carpet downstairs in the living room and dining room. The upstairs bedrooms, hallway, and steps look like they can be restored. Your budget on the house is pretty tight and you can only afford one or the other (carpet downstairs or restoring the floors upstairs). Go with the carpet in the living room and dining room.

Like I said earlier in the book, these are your money rooms. They're the first rooms the person you are showing the house to are going to see. This doesn't mean you will be neglecting the upstairs bedrooms, hallway and steps, for I have a cheaper solution for them.

Have you ever heard of carpet in a can? It's called paint. Rustoleum gray oil-based paint to be exact, and it works great. Two gallons at about $25 per gallon should do the trick. Simply roll out all the bedroom floors, the hallway and steps and you're done. The floors are restored for $50 bucks! Unless you want a high pile from your carpet in a can, that would be two coats of paint! (joke) Your floors may look like the floors of a navy battleship when you're done, but they will look clean and you will save some cash. Besides, I've done this trick to about 50 houses and have never had any complaints. In fact, some people even liked the look of it.

Kitchen and bathroom floors: The same thing goes here. If the floors are in good shape just leave them alone. Why spend money if you don't have to? Now, let's say you have to. The floors that are in the kitchen are cracked, ripped or missing tiles. Something must be done. Here's the cheapest and easiest way of replacing them. Stick down tiles! It's easy, it's cheap, I won't say it's fun but anybody with half a brain can install one. Here's how, step by step.

#1. The product you're going to be putting over your existing floor with is called Luan. It is sold at Home Depot for $10 per sheet. Simply cover your entire existing floor with Luan using underlayment nails to nail it down with. Make sure that you use underlayment nails because they are ridged at the top and they will never work themselves out. Once they're in, they're in.

#2. The stick down tiles we use are made by Images. They cost $1.25 per tile and also can be purchased at Home Depot. I have tried tile that was cheaper and I have tried tile that was more expensive, but I have found that this tile works the best. The cheaper tile is too thin, doesn't stick as good and wears out pretty quickly. The more expensive tile is harder to work with. It's a little bit thicker which makes it harder to cut, which in turn, slows you down. Also, you will wear out your razor knife blade a lot quicker. Not that blades are expensive, but if you have to stop every ten minutes to put a new blade in, the floor will take longer to install than you originally thought. Once the Luan is down, it's easy. Simply peel and stick.

#3. When you are finished with the floor, nail down a carpet bar over the edge of the door opening. This will prevent your tiles from popping up.

Ceilings: I am going to give you a couple of different scenarios here. The first is how to fix your ceilings when you first purchase the property and while it is vacant. The second scenario is when a ceiling has to be repaired while you have a tenant living in your property.

Let's get to the first scenario. You purchase a handyman special which needs some work. The property has been vacant for some time; meanwhile the roof has sprung a leak which, in turn, ruins the rear two bedroom ceilings.

Ruined bedroom ceiling

First, of course, you would have the roof repaired. Here are two options on what you can do to repair the ceiling: #1. Costly and time consuming and expensive way! Not that there's anything wrong with ripping down the old, destroyed drywall or lath, cutting and hanging new drywall, spackling and taping your joints, not once but twice, and then putting two coats of paint on the ceiling, but it takes too much damn time. You have to come back at least three different days while you wait for the spackle to dry first, then the second coat of spackle, then you have to wait for the first coat of paint to dry before you put on the second. I'm sure it will look great once you're done, but do you really have the time? Remember, every day your property sits vacant, you lose rent. Every day your property sits vacant, you run the risk of somebody breaking in.

#2. Install a dropped ceiling. It's the fastest and easiest way to go. Not to mention the cleanest. You don't have to worry about paint spilling or spackle dust from sanding going all over the house. Simply remove the hanging debris from the ceiling and install your dropped ceiling. The whole process should take you about 4 hours for one bedroom. The more you do, the faster you will get at it. I could probably snap one together in a small bedroom in about an hour and a half. Plus, they're pretty inexpensive.

Let's move on to the next scenario. All the ceilings in the property were fine when you moved your tenant in. Low and behold she clogs and overflows the toilet. Gallons of water overflow from the bowl before she is able to turn the toilet off. The water takes out your dining room ceiling. Do you spend 3 days over your tenant's house re-drywalling and painting the ceiling? No! Spend 4 hours installing a new dropped ceiling so she can overflow the toilet again next week and ruin what you just did? Hell No! I'll tell you what to do – patch it. Patch it with Luan. Cut a piece big enough to go over the hole, screw it in place, caulk around it neatly, paint it and call it a day. The whole shootin' match will take no longer than an hour, and you will pass inspection. When the tenant tells you she doesn't like the way it looks, tell her you don't like fixing things that she broke. If she wants, she can hire a contractor to fix the whole thing properly, but she will have to pay him and you know that ain't gonna happen. Her other option is an easy one. Just tell her, don't look up!

CHAPTER 10

PAINTING

After cleaning out your entire house, the next step will be to paint it. The first thing you're going to have to make a decision on is what you are going to be painting. Here's what to do. Before painting anything in the property, go from room to room and caulk all the cracks in the walls and ceilings. Also fill all nail holes with spackle. This whole process will add only about an hour to your painting but you will be glad you did it. Your paint job will turn out looking like glass.

Anything that has a natural wood finish like doors, paneling, cabinets, railings, etc., don't paint. Leave them just the way they are. Section 8 inspectors look for chipping or peeling paint and will fail you the second they find it. The first time you paint something, everything is fine and dandy. The inspector comes out, the paint is fresh and new, and you pass with flying colors. A year later, the inspector comes out and the stained bedroom door you wasted your time painting looks like it's been through hell. The paint is chipping and peeling from top to bottom. Guess what, you just failed your annual inspection. Now you have to come out to the property and paint the door again. You might even have to do it again the next year. It's not that you're using cheap paint, it's that some people don't know how to take care of things. Now, you're wishing you had never started painting the door because you don't know when you're going to stop! Will this be an annual thing or is your tenant really going to learn how to take care of the door this time around? My bet is that it will be an annual repair. Why play the guessing game! Don't paint it and you will never have to paint it again. So what if it gets old looking. As long as it opens and closes, you will never fail. The same thing applies with your paneling, cabinets, railings, etc. Section 8 will not tell you to spruce something up because it looks old. As long as it works properly, you will pass.

Now let's talk about what to do if you have to paint. The house you purchased has dark dingy walls and you want to clean it up so that you can rent it. The first thing to decide on is what type of paint you should use. Your answer should always be MAB. For those people who think that paint is paint, you're nuts. I've tried every major brand out there and none of them compare to MAB. I can cover a wall with one coat in most cases. With all the other brands I've tried, I'm lucky to cover in 2 or 3 coats. It's just like it says on the label, "Do it right the first time!"

The brand we used from MAB is Master Painters. The color we use is white semi-gloss. The white makes the house appear a little larger and white gives it a very clean look. The semi-gloss can be wiped with water if it gets dirty. We paint all of our houses the same exact color so that if someone moves out, we can either touch it up or repaint it. We don't have to try and match up what color we used on the walls because we know we always use the same product.

Anything that is metal in the property that needs painting gets painted with Rustoleum. MAB should share its marketing slogan with Rustoleum. The stuff really works great. We paint our outside railings, basement pipes, old metal kitchen cabinets that have already been painted, rusted skylights, etc. Whatever needs it, gets it.

You really won't believe what a difference a good paint job on your property will do. It may be the difference in getting your property rented quickly or slowly. Painting is not a hard thing to do and can make all the difference in the world if done properly.

We can usually pick up a 5 gallon bucket of MAB Master Painters for $50. That would be $10 per gallon. The price for a gallon of Rustoleum is $20 a gallon. You can purchase the Rustoleum nearly anywhere, Home Depot, hardware store, K-Mart, etc. MAB paint was bought by Sherwin-Williams and is now easy to find. In Volume 3 we share what paint replaced it as our go-to.

One last important thing. I know that you are going to be able to find cheaper products out there, but don't give into the temptation. You can easily paint an entire rowhome with about six gallons of MAB paint. That would cost you sixty bucks. Let's say you found a brand that cost half as much as MAB. I guarantee you that you will have to at least double coat the walls. Now you have spent exactly the same amount, but you have done twice the amount of work. Stick with a winner. And besides, why do you think they have been around so long. Quality, that's why!

CHAPTER 11

ELIMINATION

Okay, you've read every section in this book up until now. So by now, you should have a pretty good idea of what we like to eliminate from our properties. You should also have a good idea of why we eliminate these items. Believe me, none of these items were chosen at random or because we just thought it would be a good idea to eliminate them. No, unfortunately we learned the hard way. Every single item we have told you to eliminate has bitten us in the ass at least once because we did not eliminate it from our property the first time. You know the saying, "Fool me once, shame on you. Fool me twice, shame on me." That was always our motto. Once you fail an inspection for an item that a tenant destroyed, and you find out you never needed that item to begin with, you make sure that it will never happen to you again.

Fortunately for you, Nick and I have taken several hundred bullets for you. By purchasing this book you get the benefit of our years in the Section 8 field. You are going to know what to eliminate before it gets destroyed. Not only will you save money by *not* repairing things you don't need, but you will also make money by passing your inspections. Inspections are so much easier to pass when you give your tenant the bare minimum of what is needed to pass a Section 8 inspection. Your tenants are on Section 8. They are not expecting properties with dishwashers, central air, Jacuzzis, garbage disposals, etc. So why give it to them? You're not going to get paid any more than what a 2 or 3 bedroom home in the area is renting for anyway. The only thing your tenant is looking for is a home that is clean and functional. I've never had a tenant not rent a house because it didn't have a garbage disposal or dishwasher. These things are simply not expected. You could consider yourself a nice guy by not eliminating these items and leaving them there for your tenants to use. I would consider yourself a sucker when you're paying to have them repaired or replaced. You don't need 'em, they don't need 'em, they ain't getting 'em. END OF STORY!

Like I said, I've already mentioned the items we eliminate and why we eliminate them all throughout this book. In this section, I'll hit on them all one more time and give you a quick sentence or two on why we eliminate them. Kind of a refresher course, if you will. Anyway, I believe that elimination is the most important part of your turnover. Once you eliminate something the first time you will never have to eliminate it again. It's like walking through your property and picking out all the future headaches and throwing them in a trash can. It's great. I love it! I can only think of one thing I enjoy more than eliminating headaches and that is passing inspections. If you eliminate your headaches, then you will indeed pass your inspections. Let's run down these items to eliminate one more time.

Bathroom:

1. Five gallon flush toilet: replace it with a 1.6 gallon toilet. Why pay for 3.4 extra gallons of water?

2. Wall hung basin: replace it with a vanity. You will never have to worry about somebody knocking it off the wall.

3. Old leaky faucets and three handle tub diverters: replace them with single handle Moens. Knock your chances of three stems leaking down to one vinyl cartridge. If your single handle Moen leaks, simply change the cartridge. No more rusted out and/or stripped seats.

4. Caulk: Always caulk your tub before move-in. With a $2 tube of caulk, you can save hundreds of dollars in future damages caused by leaks. Also caulk around the base of the tub and the perimeter of the bathroom floor.

Bedrooms:

1. Broken doors: replace them with interior solid core doors – never hollow. For about $15 more, you will have a door that will last forever. A hollow door may not last you the duration of one tenant.

2. Ceiling fan: replace it with a globe light. If you leave a ceiling fan, it will break. Your tenant will want a new one. There will

be an argument. The price of a ceiling fan is about $50; the price of a light fixture is $10. It's an easy decision.

3. Dry rotted or destroyed carpet: replace it with nothing. Either paint the bedroom floor gray or have the hardwood refinished. Carpet is the worst investment in a rental property, hands down!

4. Closet doors: don't replace them at all. If the inside of your closet is in good shape, leave the closet doors off. If the inside of your closet is hammered, eliminate the closet. That's why they make dressers and bureaus.

Living room and dining room:

1. Dry rotted or destroyed carpet: replace it with average carpet or have the hardwood floors refinished. Although carpet is a bad investment in any rental property, it may pay dividends here. Chances are that if your flooring looks good in these two rooms, you will be able to rent your property sooner rather than later.

2. Doorbells: replace them with nothing. If you eliminate them, your tenant will never know they were there. Make a fist and knock.

Kitchen:

1. Garbage disposals: remove them. Unless you own stock in a drain cleaning company, get rid of your garbage disposal. Otherwise, you will be paying to have your kitchen drain

cleaned at least 3 times per year.

2. Dishwashers: don't replace them either. The minute they stop working (and they always stop working) your tenant will be on the phone with you telling you how much she needs her dishwasher. I guarantee you she didn't have one in the house she lived in before yours so don't do her any favors by leaving one hooked up.

Basement:

Wow, where do I start? I can probably save you some time from reading 1 through 8 by simply telling you to eliminate everything except the light, but I guess I'll walk you through the basement eliminations one more time.

1. The front basement windows: replace it with plywood and siding. This window will get broken if you leave it. If not by your tenant, then by a kid playing ball on the street. Bottom line is, nobody is going to own up to it and you will be replacing it over and over again.

2. Anything that is not part of the original basement (shelves, drywall, etc) that is screwed or nailed to the walls. Remove it all. Bring the basement down to the bare walls. A lot of these older inner-city homes get water in the basement when it rains. Wood, drywall and carpets end up getting wet and moldy. These days everybody is looking for a law suit. Mold is the newest one. If you don't have anything in the basement, nothing will get moldy.

3. Washers and dryers: take them out. If you leave them there, your tenant will use or at least attempt to use them. Your reward – high water bills from the washer and a fire hazard from the dryer.

4. Washer and dryer hook-ups: cut them, cap them and walk away. Now, if your tenants bring their own washer and dryer, they will be incapable of hooking them up. Your tenant wants to do wash – try the laundromat.

5. Washtubs: remove the washtub and trap. Cut and cap the water lines. Your tenants can wash their hands upstairs. You're also eliminating another sink that can leak or clog.

6. Front and rear hose bibs: again, cut them, cap them and walk away. Your tenant wants to fill a pool and go swimming, she can join a public pool. Your tenant wants to wash his car, he can go to the car wash.

7. Wires: any wires that are not operating something should be eliminated. A good electrician will be able to find which wires are and which wires are not live.

8. Fluorescent lighting: replace your fluorescents with a pull chain fixture. The minute your fluorescent lights burn out, your tenant will call you to tell you so. When you tell them to replace a fluorescent light bulb themselves, they are going to act like morons and tell you they don't know how. It's not that they don't know how, it's that they don't want to go out and spend $4 on a light bulb. A pull chain fixture takes up to a 100 watt bulb, can be replaced in 10 seconds, and costs about 79

cents. Also, fluorescent lights have several different things that can go wrong with them such as the ballast, the switch or the clips.

Front and rear yards:

1. Small trees, bushes, shrubbery: Get rid of it all. Cut it down. It's not going to help you rent the house any faster. More than likely, your tenants are not going to prune or trim them. Neighbors will complain when it grows into their yard and you will be lucky if you don't receive a fine because of it from the L & I inspectors.

2. Screen doors: if they're ruined, remove them. You don't need them. Why waste 2 cents repairing something that you don't need to pass an inspection and could quite possibly fail you if you don't eliminate it?

3. Awnings: if your awning is rusted and needs to be painted, remove it. Awnings are not required to pass inspections. You will only have to remove it once. If you decide to paint it, God knows how many more times you'll be performing this fun chore.

Final thought on ELIMINATION:

By now, I'm sure you've got the picture. Any extra thing that is not needed and left behind in your property is one extra item that can fail you on an inspection or cost you money to fix later down the line. Even if an item is not needed to pass a Section 8 inspection, if it is broken, you're still going to fail your inspection. The reason is it now becomes a hazard or safety issue. An old 2" × 4" that you left in the basement has a nail protruding from it, a ceiling fan is now missing a blade, drywall that you left up in the basement is now green and mildewed at the bottom from the rain, whatever the case – these are all problems that can be avoided. Believe me, the #1 thing the Section 8 inspector is looking for is safety hazards. It's his job to make sure the property is safe. The less you give him to look at, the less he will find.

If you don't need it to pass inspection, give me one good reason why you should leave it. There are none, other than you missed it or you were too lazy to remove it. These are two mistakes you don't want to make in this business.

The only money that I'm spending on repairs are the ones I need to do to continue to pass inspections. This doesn't make me a bad landlord or a slumlord – it makes me a good business man. A bad landlord or slumlord doesn't pass his inspections. Do you know why he doesn't pass? Because he's too busy spending countless money and time repairing things that he was too lazy to eliminate from his property before the tenant had a chance to move in and break. Does it make you a good landlord if you spend your time and money repairing items that you never needed to pass an inspection in the first place? Maybe, in the eyes of your tenants! Hell, they would have you over their house 40 hours a week repairing things if it was up to them. You know the drill, they break it, you fix it. To them you would be the best landlord in the world. To me, you would be the biggest jackass in the world. You would also be a horrible business man and my bet, you would be out of business shortly.

Eliminate, innovate, and prosper! Do it right the first time and never look back. It will get to be like a cookie cutter. The minute you open the door to the property after settlement, you'll know exactly what items must be removed. Not only will you enjoy eliminating them, but you will probably get a few good laughs while doing so. Nick and I always did! What were we laughing at you ask? Future headaches and repairs simply being tossed in a trash can or thrown on back of our stake body and being hauled to the dump. The more creative we got at eliminating things, the harder we laughed. So be creative, have fun, and always remember, a useless item eliminated today is a penny and a headache saved tomorrow!

Me(r) and Nick(l) throwing future headaches on the stake body

CHAPTER 12

WHERE ADVERTISE YOUR "PROPERTY FOR RENT"

You would think that anywhere would be a good place to advertise a home for rent. The more exposure, the better and quicker chance you have of renting your property. However, you may be placing your property in danger. You may be giving a thief a map to your property! What's their treasure? Anything they can get their hands on if they can get into your property: copper, carpets, light fixtures, heaters, stoves, etc.

Want to know how to prevent it? First, never hang a "For Rent" sign in the window. Not only are you advertising that your property is for rent, you are advertising that it is vacant. You might as well write on the back of the sign, "Thiefs, could you please lock the door on your way out!" Like they say, "Locks only keep the honest people out." If a crook knows no one is living in the property and he wants to get in, believe me, he will get in. Hell, he might even stay over a night or two. Bag the "For Rent" signs!

Next, if you are advertising your property for rent in the paper or elsewhere, never put down the full property address. Once again, you are giving a map right to the front door of your vacant property.

So let's say you have a property at 6350 Wheeler Street and you want to advertise it in the paper. Here's how to write it up:

Property for Rent

3 bedroom-Section 8 O.K.

63xx block of Wheeler

call Mike @: 555-1212

We found that, for us, advertising in the paper works well. In most cities, there is a community paper that is delivered to home owners for free. It comes out once a week or once every two weeks. Advertising in this paper is pretty cheap and the ad always generates a lot of calls. Most of the calls you get will be from people living in the area who want to stay in the area. This works well because if they wish to see the property, they already know the area and can probably meet you there within 15 minutes.

If you wish to spend a little more to get more volume from your ad, you can place your home in the city paper (Philadelphia Daily News for us). Not only will it generate more calls, it will also bring in people from outside the area you are renting in. Not that this is a bad thing but having to give exact directions to 50 people who are coming from 50 different directions can be a pain in the ass. Also, if they tell you they will be at your property in a half an hour, it might take them 50 minutes depending on traffic. You want to give them the benefit of the doubt by not leaving because they are coming from far away or may have gotten lost. More importantly than giving them the benefit of the doubt is that you want to get your property rented, so you usually end up waiting. Now you've wasted 20 minutes sitting in front of your home. It's worth it if the prospective tenant says they want to rent it, but if not, you wasted time, and time is money in this business.

Another way of getting the property rented that works very well is to advertise at your Section 8 office. There are two ways of doing this and number one is very simple. If your branch has a cork board (all Philadelphia branches do), simply pin your ad to it.

If your rental property has a nice kitchen or bath, take a picture of it and include it with your ad. Once again, you won't have to give your exact address of the property which is good. Also, you will be guaranteeing yourself that the person answering your ad will be a Section 8 tenant.

Number two is also very simple, but it has its good side and bad side. All Section 8 offices have a form which you can fill out to advertise the listing of your property. Simply go to the front desk and ask for a "listing form."

Your property, along with other landlord's properties, will be printed out and distributed to Section 8 participants who are looking for a home. The good side is that your ad will reach many people, all of whom will be on Section 8. The bad side is that Section 8 requires you to give the full property address. If you can't get the property rented by any of the other ways, you may have to bite the bullet and give out the address. Desperate times call for desperate measures.

These are the ways we have found to be most successful, but hey, if you want to get creative and can think of better or quicker ways of renting your property, then knock yourself out! The bottom line is to get it rented. Empty boxes don't make any money!

CHAPTER 13

SECURING YOUR PROPERTY WHILE VACANT

Most of the inner-city streets where you will be purchasing your rental properties are going to be rather small and, of course, rowhomes are close together. Not that this is a bad thing, but the neighbors will be able to see everything that you are doing while rehabbing your property. They will be able to see what new items you put into the property such as a new stove, carpets, cabinets, etc. To someone living three doors down with hardwood floors and a 30-year-old stove with only one operable burner, you can see how appealing some of your new upgrades would look in their home rather than yours. Ninety-five percent of the time, no one will even attempt to break into your home. Now let's discuss the other 5% and some tips on securing your property.

You can usually eliminate anyone breaking in through the upstairs. Not too many people are going to carry a 25' ladder up the street to attempt to break in. If you have a porch roof with windows above it – now that's a different story.

Somebody who lives on the same side of the street can walk the porch roofs to your house and test the upper windows. Be sure they are locked, and if you still don't feel comfortable, place a screw in one or both sides of the window.

If your property has a skylight in the bathroom, just make sure it is closed. Out of all the houses we have owned, we have never had anyone even attempt to break in through the skylight and, believe me, we have seen it all.

The downstairs windows are the same as the upstairs. Make sure they are locked and, again, if you don't feel comfortable enough, put a screw or two in them. Also, if you are in the process of rehabbing the home and you have some plywood or paneling laying around, simply lean the wood over the front and back windows.

This won't prevent anybody from breaking into the property, but it may prevent them from trying. Ya see, if a thief can look right into your property, he may see something he likes. If he sees something he likes, he may attempt to break in.

If your property has a back door (usually in the kitchen) make sure you have a good lock (Kwikset) on it. If it is a wooden door, you can screw a 3" screw through the door and into the doorjamb. One at the top and one near the bottom should do the trick.

If your property has a steel door, cut a 30 inch 2" by 4" and screw it to the floor behind the door.

The only thing that you should have left in the downstairs is the front door. The only thing that you can do to prevent a break-in here is use a good quality lock. You can't screw the front door shut because you would be locking yourself out. Most thieves do not want to come through the front door anyway because of the likelihood of being spotted. The front of the home is visible from people walking outside, police driving down the street and also the neighbors in their homes.

The last thing that you have to secure is the basement. In the "Elimination" chapter, I showed you how we eliminate all basement windows except for one. You only need one window in the basement to pass inspection.

Not only does doing this eliminate the risk of the window getting broken, it also eliminates break-ins while the unit is vacant. You should only have one window in the basement and if that window is a hopper or slider, you're in good shape. Not only do they have an extremely strong lock, but they are small and chances are a thief would not be able to fit through the window if he succeeds in getting it open.

If your property has a basement door, here's what to do. Whether the door is wood or steel, it's going to have a wooden frame. Measure from jamb to hinge side and cut a 2" × 4" this length. Screw the 2" × 4" across the door and into the jamb, and your job is done.

Everybody has heard the saying that if somebody wants to get into your property bad enough, they will. I also believe this. But the longer a thief tries to get into your property, the better chance he will be spotted or caught. You might even discourage him enough into walking away.

CHAPTER 14

SHOWING YOUR PROPERTY

Okay, your property is completely rehabbed, you have received several calls from prospective tenants, and you want to begin showing the property. What do you do now?

First, it all starts with the phone. You can eliminate 60% of the callers by asking them, "Are you on Section 8?" If their answer is "No," tell them you will take their number down and call them back. They're eliminated. About 40% of your other calls will be from Section 8 participants who will answer "Yes, I am on Section 8." You can also eliminate about half of these callers by asking, "Do you have your packet?" A packet is the paperwork they will give you to fill out if they chose your property. Tell them you can't show them your property without the packet. The reason for this is as follows. If they have their packet in hand, they are ready to move. You can fill it out for them, have them bring it back to Section 8, and you will probably get an inspection date in about a week. Also, if they have their packet and don't bring it with them, you will have to meet them again to fill it out. Make sure they have it in their hands before you open the door, otherwise, you're just wasting time. If a prospective tenant is on Section 8, wants to see your property, and tells you they will be getting their packet soon, again, you are wasting time. Tenants have to go through several different steps when moving from one property to another in order to be issued a new packet. Some of the steps include: giving their landlord sixty days written notice, notifying their Section 8 service rep, getting re-evaluated, etc. A tenant who comes to your property with packet in hand has already done all of this and is ready to go. Don't feel as though you are losing out by turning down a Section 8 participant who doesn't have their packet. Believe me, there are plenty of people who are already ready to go.

The ones without the packet will tell you the craziest things like, "I have to give my landlord 60 days notice that I am moving so can you hold the property for me?" Yeah, right lady. I'm gonna lose two months of rent waiting for you! I don't think so! They're not ready to move and they're just out wasting landlord's time shopping for something better.

Now, you're down to about 20% of your callers who have a packet and are ready to go. Be sure that if you are renting out a 3 bedroom home your caller has a three bedroom packet. Some participants think that if they have a 2 bedroom packet, they can move into a 3 bedroom home. WRONG! They will if you let them, but you're only costing yourself money. Here's why.

Let's say that these are the fair market rents in the neighborhood you are renting in:

#1) 2 bedroom home @ $650 per month

#2) 3 bedroom home @ $750 per month

#3) 4 bedroom home @ $850 per month

The home that you are renting is a 3 bedroom home so you would like to get $750 a month for it. The caller who answered your ad has a two bedroom packet. The most you can get from her would be $650. This is what she has been allotted for by Section 8. Her packet does not have enough value for her to rent a 3 bedroom home. On the other hand, if you are renting a 3 bedroom home and the participant has a 4 bedroom packet, this packet will have more than enough value to get you your $750 asking price. Most tenants will tell you that their Section 8 service rep told them they can go up one bedroom size, but that doesn't mean you're going to get paid for it. It's a landlord's decision and unless you like losing $100 per month in rent, it should be an easy decision at that.

It always amazed Nick and I that someone who is getting a house for free also wants an extra bedroom. If you were starving and someone gave you a hotdog, would you ask for fries too? No, you would be happy with what you were given. Believe me, some of these people have brass balls and as long as you give them things, they will continue to ask.

Ask the tenant to show you her voucher. It will say whether she has a 2, 3, 4 bedroom packet.

Finally, you have narrowed down your callers to possibly eight people who have in their possession a 3 bedroom packet. Schedule

137

different times for each person to view your home. **<u>Never</u>** hold an open house. An open house would be if you called all eight people and told them you are showing the house on Saturday, June 5th at 2:00 pm You would probably get your house rented but you more than likely will have to break up 2 or 3 fights. You might as well wear a referee shirt! If there is more than one person who would like to rent your property, be prepared for one of them to say they saw it first, they called you first, etc. Once you make a decision, the person you didn't pick may want to fight you!

Here's what to do. Simply space out your showings a half an hour apart. Bring the list of names and phone numbers of who is coming and when. Let's say the second person to look at the home wants to rent it. Fill out their packet and call the others on your list to cancel. Tell them you will keep their number and if you get anything else, you will call them back. At least, if they try to start a fight with you over the phone, you can hang up!

Here are some tips on what to do and what not to do when showing a prospective tenant your home:

a. Make sure they have their packet in hand.
b. Check to see that it's the proper bedroom size.
c. Open the door, stand in the living room and tell them they are free to check out the property.
d. Do not follow them around; it's an empty house so feel at ease. Besides, if you follow them around, you'll get bombarded with questions. Sure, they are going to ask you questions, but they

might forget half of them by the time they get back up or down the steps.

e. Answer 'no' to all the questions. "No, I'm not painting the living room red." "No, I'm not putting down new carpet." "No, I'm not replacing the stove." "No, I'm not putting in an alarm system." "No, no, no!" When you finished your rehab of the property, that's just what you did – finished! You made up your mind and felt comfortable that your property would rent and pass Section 8 inspection. Don't let a tenant tell you what will and will not pass inspection. Most of the time, the things they want you to replace are cosmetic and only for their own gain. Tell them if they don't rent it, somebody else will and move on to the next person on your list.

f. If a prospective tenant tells you that they like the property but they want to look at one more and then they'll call you back, keep showing it. Don't consider it rented until you have filled out someone's packet. Hopefully, if she calls you back, you can tell her the good news that the property has already been rented. It's like a sign I once saw in a car dealership that read, "The car you said you would come back for tomorrow is the car that somebody came back for today!"

g. If the person wants your property, fill out her packet. Call her the next day to see if she has returned the packet to Section 8. If so, wait for the phone to ring for your inspection date.

h. After the tenant leaves your property, go around to check and see if all the windows and doors are locked. I can't tell you how many times a tenant has opened the basement door to look at the rear yard and forgot to lock it.

CHAPTER 15

MOVE IN DAY

Finally! You have renovated your property, rented it to a Section 8 participant, passed the inspection, signed the leases, and received your security deposit. You're about to start getting some return on your investment. You only have to jump through one more hoop. Move in day!

It sounds pretty easy. Give them your phone number, two sets of keys, wish them luck and be on your way. If these are the only 3 things you do on move in day, you're the guy that's going to need the luck. There's a lot more to it than that. Let's go over move in day, in order, step by step.

#1. If your property has a front lawn, while walking to the front door with them, politely mention that you don't do landscaping and it is up to them to keep the grass cut. Also tell them that when it snows they have to shovel the snow. (All of this will be in their lease but, who knows if they will read it. Save yourself the phone call of "When are you coming over to cut my grass?")

#2. After opening the front door, give them their two sets of keys. Tell them to make more copies if they need them. Tell them they are not allowed to change any of the locks on the property. Tell them the first time they change a lock on your property will be the last. Changing locks is cause for eviction. Also, tell them they will have to call a locksmith if they get locked out. Tell them to give a copy of the key to a parent or friend and to call them if they are locked out, not you!

#3. After you open the door of the property, the first question the tenant usually asks is "Do you mind if we paint?" Early on, when we first started out, I would say, "No, go right ahead." Even if I had just had the place painted, I figured, hey, if you want to change some colors around, knock yourself out! Besides if they are painting, that shows some enthusiasm that they want to spruce up and take care of the place. However, that's not always the case. First of all, 99% of the time, their choice of colors are horrible. Not that I'm an interior decorator or give two shits about what color the bedroom walls are, but come on, bright red? Pumpkin orange? Violet and hunter green? Do you know how many coats of primer it takes to paint over a purple wall? Not only that, but they get paint all over the carpets or floor. I don't think they ever heard of drop cloths. Anyway, the answer is no, they can't paint. The color of the walls they came in with are the colors they will go out with.

Remember, you're still trying to be nice here. Nice, but firm. You're just letting them know it's your house and your rules. You don't have to get nasty with them because they haven't done anything wrong, *yet*. Who knows, they might even end up being a very good tenant. Right now they are just testing you with questions, seeing if they can get anything extra out of you. The first time you say yes to a question, they will ask you ten more. Here's a line I like to use after the first question, "Mrs. Green, I did what I had to do to pass the Section 8 inspection. I won't be doing anything else." Once they see you're not willing to give an inch, they will stop asking questions. Don't beat around the bush and give them a chicken shit answer like, "I don't know, I'll have to ask my partner about getting you some new screens," or "Let's see how long you stay and I might be able to give you new carpet." Believe me, they'll be on the phone with you the next day asking you when you're bringing over the new screens. Three months later, they'll be on the phone with you saying, "I've been here three months, where's my carpet?" The answer to their demands is always NO.

#4. Getting back to the move in tour, once your in the property, proceed upstairs. Show them where the smoke detectors are and tell them that it's a tenant's responsibility to keep them working at all times. A battery costs 89 cents, so change it.

#5. The first room you will go into upstairs is the bathroom. Walk over to the toilet and flush it. Once you and your tenant see the water go down, it's no longer your responsibility. Tell them the line is clear now and if it gets clogged, they must unclog it. Tell them to make sure they buy or already own a plunger because you won't be coming out for **any** clogs. Here's a line I like to use. "The sewer line is clear now, so if it gets clogged, it's on you. I can't clog it from my house, so it's

143

something you put down the toilet. The same goes for the tub and the vanity." Fill them with some water, pull the plug and watch the water go down.

#6. Let them look at the bedrooms. There shouldn't be any kind of friction here. Proceed downstairs to the kitchen.

#7. Take them over to the kitchen sink, fill it, and let the water go down. Walk over to the stove and turn on all the burners. Let them know that all four are working properly right now because they are all clean. The number one reason burners stop working is because grease clogs the gas portholes. Tell them to keep the stove clean and they won't have any problems.

#8. Go down the basement. In the plumbing section we told you we install a new 3/4" ball valve in all of our houses. Walk the tenant directly over to it. Show them the on and off positions. Tell them that if there is any kind of leak or pipe break to go directly to this ball valve and shut it off. Tell them that it will shut down all the water coming into the house.

I've had pipes break and the tenant would call me or the water company instead of turning off the water. Let her know that if she doesn't shut it off, she will be held accountable for the damage the water caused as well as the excess water bill. This is also in our lease.

Next walk them over to the water heater and house heater. Tell them that once they get the gas turned on, the gas man will be lighting the pilot on both the heater and water heater. When he does, tell your tenant to pay attention because you don't come out to light pilots. It's not a hard thing to do and the directions are right on the side of the heater or water heater. If my 65-year-old mother can do it, so can they.

#9. Wish them luck, give them your phone number to your office (never your cell phone) and be on your way. Hopefully, you won't be seeing or hearing from them until your next Section 8 inspection.

There is one more thing that I would like to add to this section that I feel is very important. Before the tenant takes possession of the house, videotape the condition of the entire home. The whole process will only take about five minutes, but it could be the most important five minutes you spend on the house. Should the tenant destroy the home, you will have proof that he or she is responsible for the damage.

The next thing you want to do is take a picture of each and every room in the home. You're probably asking, "Why do you need a picture if you already video recorded the home?" The answer is because you're going to have your tenant sign the back of each and every picture. When you walk her into the master bedroom, show her the picture of the master bedroom and have her sign it. When you show her the bathroom, give her the picture of the bathroom and have her sign it. You get the picture?

Not only will this add to your proof because their signature is on the back of each picture, but it may also deter them from wrecking the place. Tell them that you have a video recording of the entire place before they moved in and this is how you want your property to look when they move out. I also like to use this line: "I'm not the kind of landlord who lets you wreck my house and move onto the next. If you wreck this house, believe me, you won't be getting another. I will fight my hardest to get your Section 8 packet revoked."

Now after hearing this, signing pictures, and being told that you videotaped the entire property, the tenant will know that you are very serious about them keeping your property in good order. Just planting a threatening seed about getting them kicked off Section 8 will go a long way. Speak up, it's your house!

CHAPTER 16

KEEPING YOUR TENANT

After reading this book up to this point, by now you've got to be thinking, "My god, this guy is at war with his tenants. He hates them!" That's not the case. I'm just giving you important information and ideas on what to do when *bad* tenants rent your property. Do you really need any information on good tenants other than how to keep them in your property? I don't know any landlords pulling their hair out saying, "I'm so confused on what to do with all these good tenants of mine." That's because the answer is quite simple. Keep them in your property.

What is a good Section 8 tenant? Well, I know a lot of guys who are in the same business as me and all will agree on the same things.

1. **They pay their rent on time, every time.** I'm not one for excuses and Nick is worse. Especially when you are playing with our money. The rent money is why you are in this game and it's how you make a living. I hate hearing the polite way of someone asking you if they can screw you over for a little

while longer. You know the one, "I don't have the rent right now, can you work with me?" Your response to this question should be, "My mortgage company doesn't work with me so I'm not gonna work with you!" Let them know the very first time they give you an excuse that you won't tolerate late rent, otherwise, you'll get an excuse every month. A soft heart is the quickest way to an empty wallet.

2. **If any of the utilities are in their name, they don't abuse them.** Section 8 has a set amount of what they will pay you if you decide to leave a water bill, gas bill, or electric bill in your name. Here is a chart of what Section 8 pays for a certain utility in Philadelphia.

So let's say your tenant is living in a 2 bedroom unit. You are paying the water bill. Section 8 gives you $38 extra per month for water. The tenant's water bill stays at or below this amount. That's a good tenant. If the bills are continuously higher than this amount, then they are cutting into your wallet. That's not a good tenant.

Here's a little something off the record that pertains to #3 that might help you sleep a little better. When I first got started in this business and owned under 10 homes, I would get sick and or really mad if I went into one of my properties and saw that it was a mess. Dishes stacked 2 foot high in the sink, laundry all over the house, stains on the carpets, etc. I would snap at the tenants, give them 24 hours to clean it up or I would be calling Section 8 and evicting them. For 24 hours, my stomach would burn, I would be in a pissed off mood, and I would be awake for half the night. The next day when I would return to inspect the "clean up" of the property, I would usually only get sicker. They would do a half assed job of cleaning up. They would jam junk in the closet, run the vacuum, spray some air freshener, light an incense, take out the trash and call it a day. Just enough to shut me up. Ten to one odds the house would look the way it did the day before within a half an hour of me leaving.

Once we owned over 10 homes, I finally got it through my thick head, THIS IS A BUSINESS. If you stay up at night worrying about which tenant is taking out the trash or doing the dishes, you ain't gonna make it in this field. There's more important things to worry about like purchasing more properties, getting them rented, and building your own empire!

Now, I look back and laugh about the things I used to worry about. What the hell was I worried about dirty dishes in a sink for? I was getting paid on the property every month! Nowadays, getting paid is the only thing that I worry about and, believe me, my worries are few and far between.

3. **They don't destroy your property.** By destroying, I mean smashing holes in walls, kung fu-ing doors in half or off the hinges, ripping cabinet doors off hinges, etc. – you get the picture. However, here is an important tip: Don't get destruction mixed up with poor housekeeping. Poor housekeeping I can deal with. You don't have to live there; them being dirty isn't costing you a cent, and when Section 8 inspects the property, housekeeping is a tenant's job. They

can't stop paying you because your tenant is a slob. Destruction is another story.

4. **You don't hear from them on a monthly basis.** They don't bother you for every little thing that is cracked or loose in the house. They don't call the Section 8 inspector out for a "tenant complaint". A tenant complaint is when your tenant decides to go above your head and call Section 8 out to the property to inspect something that they feel they need or for something that needs to be repaired. Your property only needs to be inspected by Section 8 once per year to stay on the payroll, so ideally, this is what you want. All landlords would gladly not hear from the tenant all year until the next inspection date rolls around. You get your inspection report, do the repairs, and you're good for another year. Kind of like a car inspection. Can you imagine how pissed you would be if half way through your inspection your mechanic called you and said, "Hey, Mike, can you bring your car back in and let me get another look at it?"

5. **No calls from neighbors or police.** Although you may not hear from your tenants (which is good) you may hear from neighbors who live next to your tenants, or from the police! They're called "nuisance calls" and whoever made up that name for them really hit the nail on the head. I have no idea how neighbors or police get a hold of my phone number, but they do. They want to give you an earful of what your tenant is doing and what they're going to do if it doesn't stop. I will give my tenants a call and warn them to knock off whatever it is

they are doing over there, but I don't worry too much about these calls. A lot of neighbors find out that the property is being rented Section 8 and get a little bit too excited when they see or hear things coming from the property. What I do worry about is neighbors calling Section 8 and complaining about a certain property. Why do I worry more about neighbors calling Section 8 more than I worry about them calling the police? *CASSSHHH!* Section 8 can terminate a tenant's packet for numerous complaints and/or incidents at a property. No packet, no pay. The police cannot stop your pay nor can they arrest you.

If you are renting your property to a Section 8 tenant and you have these 5 things going your way, what more could you ask for? Good housekeeping? That would be a bonus. Anyway, a tenant who is giving you these 5 things would be considered a good tenant in my eyes. Do your best to keep them in your property because, if they move out, not only do you have to get the property rented and inspected again, you also run the risk of a bad tenant taking a good tenant's place. A property that you were used to going over to once or twice a year now becomes a headache.

What do you do to keep them happy and staying in your property? Not much, but a little is all right. Usually, I will give them something that benefits me or my property. Never anything cosmetic.

If a tenant has been with me for, say five years, rarely calls me, and her home usually passes inspection, I might be inclined to go the extra yard. Let's say her 15-year-old stove is not working. I will send an appliance repair man over and he tells me the repairs on the stove will cost $160. Well, hell, a new stove only costs me $240. I would call the tenant and say, "Mrs. Green, I could repair your stove, but since you're one of my *good* tenants, I'm going to get you a new one." They will thank you and hopefully you won't hear from them for another three years! Not only is the tenant happy, but now you have a new stove in your property that shouldn't give you any problems for the next 10 years. It is items like this, items that you will need in the property for years to come, that I will make an upgrade on for a *good* tenant. Had she been a bad tenant, I would have looked in the Trade-n-Times and found a gas stove for $75. Her 15-year-old stove may have been replaced with a 16-year-old stove that works.

Being a landlord, many times you have to wear several different hats. In this case, you would be putting on your accountant's hat. Should I spend $240 on a stove for a bad tenant who might grease it up and by the time they move out, the stove looks like it's 15 years old? If that's the case, should I just give the appliance guy $160 to fix the 15-year-old stove that is already in place and hold my breath that the stove stays working until the bad tenant moves out? Will I be able to find a cheap working stove in the paper? A good tenant makes these decisions easier for you. If you know your property and the items inside of it are being treated properly, make the upgrade. It's as simple as that.

Now, what you can't do when you get a good tenant in the property is bend over backwards for them. Let's say they have been living in the property for 2 years. They take care of the property, it's always clean and they pass their inspections. Your phone rings and it's your tenant on the other line with a question they would like to ask you. "Mr. Mike, you know I have been taking care of your property since I moved in, right?"

"Correct," I answer.

"Well, since I'm a good tenant of yours, I would like to get some new carpet in here, could you replace it?"

Let's say carpet for the living room, dining room and hallway will run you $1,200. What are you supposed to do? I keep **my** house clean but I don't see the mortgage company at my door with any prizes or rewards. Think of it this way; if you walked into your property and the tenant had done $1,200 worth of damage, would you be irate? Of course you would! You would have to spend $1,200 of your money to fix the problem. So what's the difference – if you're spending $1,200 on repairs or on new carpet? It's still your money that you're spending. New carpet won't help you pass any inspections. It is a cosmetic upgrade that's only making one person happy – **your tenant!**

Take your wife out to a $100 dinner 12 different times and make yourself happy. Had it been a positive upgrade such as a new heater, water heater, roof, etc., you may not have been happy paying for the upgrade, but you know it would have been money well spent. The point I am trying to get across is that it's a judgment call and you shouldn't spend money in the wrong places. If the repair or upgrade benefits you, you're spending it in the right place. If it benefits the tenant, you spent it in the wrong place. A smile on my tenant's face is not worth $1,200. Telling them you won't be replacing any carpet should put a smile on yours.

CHAPTER 17

PROTECTING YOURSELF WHILE WORKING ON YOUR PROPERTY

Most of the time when you are rehabbing your property, neighbors or passersby will ask you if you're renting or selling the property. If you say you're renting the property, some might ask you if they can see inside the property. I'd say about 90% have good intentions on possibly wanting to rent your property, the other 10% have bad intentions. What could be their bad intentions? Seeing what you're putting into the property so they can come back later to rip you off. Checking to see what kind of tools are on your jobsite such as a break, table saw, etc. Looking for an opening, such as an old basement door lock or a rotted door frame, something that you haven't repaired yet that they can sneak their way in through later. Or the worse case scenario, sweet talking their way into your property, then pulling a gun and robbing you!

How can you know which 10% are the ones that are up to no good? How can you prevent them from entering your home? It's easy – keep them all out! The good and the bad – all 100%. Nobody gets in until the property is completely rehabbed and you have run an ad in the paper. If someone is looking in the paper for a home for rent, you know they're serious about renting. Who knows what somebody is up to who happens to be just wondering by?

The answer to the question, "Are you selling or renting?" is, "I don't know what the guy is going to do, I'm just the contractor. I can give you his number and you can call and ask him yourself." By answering the question in this form, you're doing yourself two favors. Number one, you're leaving the door open if the passerby did really want to rent the property. If they call and would like to see the property and have a Section 8 packet, fine, show it to them. Number two, you're preventing them from thinking that you are the owner or landlord of the property. When some of these people hear that you're the owner or landlord, they automatically think you have lots of money. That may be the case, but you don't want them knowing it. No offense to the contractors out there but 99% of people think that a landlord has deeper pockets than a contractor. The 1% who know the truth are the contractors. Anyway, you are more likely to get stuck up if you're telling the whole neighborhood that you are the landlord. Keep your mouth shut, tell them nothing and complete your project. He that speaks much is much mistaken!

Locking your doors – It amazes me when I drive by a house being rehabbed and the idiots working on it have the front door and windows wide open, the radio blaring, saw horses, wood and sometimes even tools out front. Where are they? Out back or perhaps on the roof? Who knows? But wherever they are, they're not out front with the materials. Anything can and will walk away if you're not watching it. I've also heard stories of thieves walking right into the house and walking off with a screw gun or saw. Where were the workers? In the basement pardging the walls? The only way they would have caught the guy is if he would have unplugged the radio that was blaring away in the kitchen and taken that too!

I know that you have to bring materials through the front door but the minute they're in the home, shut and lock the front door. It will prevent thieves and nosey people from looking or walking into your property. Any wood that you have to cut, don't cut it out front, use the basement. If you have a fenced in yard, cut it out there.

Here's another tip. If you hear somebody knocking on the front door, never open it. Nick and I know a contractor who did, and he was greeted with a brick to his face. Turns out he had parked his work van a little too close to the guy's BMW. If someone's knocking at the front door, go into the master bedroom, open the window and yell down, "Can I help you?" You will be able to see who's at the door and ask what they want, see what's in their hands, and most importantly turn them away. I'm not trying to scare you, but sometimes bad things can happen if you're not prepared. Always be safe rather than sorry.

Final thought on protecting yourself – When we started this business, I applied for and received a license to carry a firearm. I knew I was going to be working in the city and thought if push ever came to shove, I didn't want to come up short. I wanted to be the guy doing the pushing and/or shoving if I was ever put in that situation. Fortunately, that situation has never come about (knock on wood). Granted, I've been involved in numerous arguments and disagreements, but I've never felt threatened enough to have to draw my gun. But I'll tell you this, it's nice to know that if you need it, it's there. I'm not a hot-headed guy, so carrying a firearm works for me. Nick on the other hand, has a shorter fuse than me. A license to carry a gun probably wouldn't have been a good idea for him, therefore, he never applied. He's also 6' tall and 300 lbs, so not too many people are going to want to challenge or argue with him anyway.

You know what kind of person you are. If you're very hot headed, you get into a lot of arguments or disagreements, and you could see yourself telling someone you're going to shoot them because they wrecked your home, then maybe this isn't the route for you.

One more thing I'm going to add to *keeping your doors locked.* Another person you will be preventing from entering the property is city inspectors. If an inspector is driving down the street and sees extension cords running out the front door and plywood being cut on the lawn, he may stop to see if you have any permits for the work that's being performed. Had the front door been closed and locked, he would have never stopped. Be smart, think smart, and most of all be safe. Owning 1,000 homes is not worth your life.

CHAPTER 18

CREATING AN LLC – HOW TO, WHEN TO & WHY

The answer to these 3 questions, in order are, very easily, immediately, and so you don't get sued up the ass! In this section, we're going to give you all the legal mumbo jumbo of what an LLC is, what a corporation is, and what a partnership is. We're also going to give you what the benefits of each are, what the drawbacks are, and what is needed for start-up. The more involved legal information in this section is written by a man much more knowledgeable than I in this field. His name is Jim Bennett. You may remember his name from the banking section of this book. He is the owner and President of Stonehedge Funding. Before we get into Jim's analysis of how an LLC, corporation or partnership work, let me give you mine. Although Jim's analysis is very easy to understand and pretty self-explanatory, mine, a fourth grader would be able to understand. Kind of like an 'LLC for Idiots' version. Anyway, here goes.

When Nick and I first got involved in this business, we knew nothing about LLCs, corporations, etc. We took title as "Tenants in Common", purchased home owners insurance that gave us a $50,000 fire policy and $1,000,000 worth of liability insurance. Then we kept our fingers crossed and hoped for the best. We assumed that if the property burned down and was a complete loss, we would collect $50,000. If somebody was injured in our property and sued us, we were covered. We got lucky, very, very lucky. Although we did have one fire, no one was injured. We collected $50,000 from the fire policy and we lived happily ever after. Boy, did we ever dodge a bullet.

Here is a worse-case scenario of what could have happened that night of the fire. The fire that started in our property could have spread to the homes on both sides of ours. I've seen rowhome fires where nine or more homes in a row were taken out (look up MOVE on Osage Avenue in Philadelphia, 1985!) Not only could other homes have been destroyed by the fire, but people could have been injured or killed. Once the smoke clears, the next place you're gonna be is in court. Now, you've got eight houses to replace and, let's say, God forbid, two people dead. How far is your one million dollar liability policy going to go? Not very far. You will have enough to replace the houses but not the lives. You know the families are going to sue you and they have every right. If I lost a family member due to a fire from a Section 8 property two doors away, I would do the same, **and I am a Section 8 landlord.** You can just about guarantee the judge passing out an award of at least $5,000,000 against you. Like I said in the beginning of this section, we *only* had a $1,000,000 liability policy. Had this scenario played out, Nick and I would have been on the hook for the other four million dollars.

I didn't have four million dollars. Nick didn't have four million dollars. But we did, at that time, own 175 properties; 175 unprotected properties that is! That's because when we purchased the properties, we took title as Michael McLean and Nick Cipriano, "Tenants in Common." It would have done us just as much good if we would have taken title as Jerkoff #1 and Jerkoff #2 because that's what we were. We had 175 properties out there with no protection. Had the scenario I'm speaking of unfolded, all 175 properties would have had a lien attached to them. We were also leaving the door open for our *primary residences* to be liened on. What we had worked so hard to acquire would all have been lost. The minute we would sell a property, somebody else's hand would have been out to collect the check. Pretty scary stuff, huh? Well, thank God on our part it never happened, but you may not be so lucky. That's why you have to protect yourself by covering your ASSets. All the time, every time!

Now, by scaring you half to death with that nightmare of a scenario, I hope I got your attention. I told you how you could lose everything, now I'm gonna tell you how to keep everything. I'm going to give it to you in English and make it very easy to understand because, to be honest with you, the first time an LLC was explained to me, it was like Einstein talking to Howdy Doody. I walked away from the conversation knowing less than what I knew about an LLC before the conversation started.

I'm a slow learner when it comes to legal stuff and lawyer legalities. I can take a rundown rowhome and have it rehabbed and ready to pass a Section 8 inspection in less than a week, but give me a ten page chapter to read on corporations and LLCs and it will take me about a month to make sense of it. That's why I'm writing this section for you – so you will get it the first time you read it. I'd also like to say this in my defense – I don't think I am any less intelligent than the lawyers who write these books on LLCs and corporations. In fact, I think I'm more intelligent. Like I said, give me a 10 page chapter to read and I <u>will</u> make sense of it in one month. Put a lawyer in a rundown rowhome and tell them to get it ready to pass a Section 8 inspection and it <u>won't</u> happen. Not in a day, not in a month, not in a year! Does it make me more intelligent that I can pick up their line of work in one month and they couldn't pick up my line of work if their life depended on it? I'd say so! There's a saying Nick's mom used to say about someone who was very well educated but not too handy or street smart. She'd call them an 'educated asshole.' I just figured I'd throw this paragraph out there for any lawyers who were reading this section and were starting to feel pretty intelligent about themselves. It's not that I don't like lawyers but, ahh, what the hell, you caught me, I don't like lawyers. (Exceptions to the Perpiglia Brothers!) Every business book has a lawyer joke – why not mine!

Anyway, let's get back to the business at hand. Explaining an LLC in layman's terms by Michael McLean. I'm not going to give you the legalities of it such as taxation, corporate formalities, exact cost (although very cheap), etc. What I'm simply going to do is show you how it can protect you. That's it. That's really all you want and need to know. Once you make the determination that an LLC or corporation is right for you, contact a lawyer, pay him what it costs to set it up and you're protected. Your worries about somebody else owning what you have worked for are over and done with.

Here's how it works! Let's make it easy. Let's say you own six properties in the city of Philadelphia. Let's say they are all on the same street.

You could put each of your homes in its own individual LLC. Since it costs about $500 to set up each LLC, you could see where this might get a little expensive. What Nick and I did was put 2 homes into each LLC, essentially cutting the costs in half. You can put as many homes as you like into each LLC, but the more you put in, the less your protection becomes. Here's why. Let's say you own the six properties I have listed above and create 3 LLCs. Each LLC consists of two properties; 2601 and 2605 Hobson are entered into an LLC which you name "Red Dog LLC," 2610 and 2618 Hobson are entered into an LLC in which you name "Blue Dog LLC," lastly 2631 and 2633 Hobson are entered into an LLC which you name "Yellow Dog LLC." You will purchase a home owner's policy which covers each LLC separately. Now, instead of having a $50,000 fire policy, you bump it up to $100,000. Remember, your now covering two houses. You may be able to get away with a $50,000 fire policy, but if that one in a million shot that both your houses in the LLC burn down on the same night, you're shit outta luck and, more importantly, you're out $50,000. Remember, you're covering your ASSets. Take no chances. However, you will be able to keep the $1,000,000 liability clause in check. The reason for this is simple. No matter what happens to this LLC or that LLC, the most anybody is going to be able to sue you for is the amount of liability insurance you purchased. Once the insurance is done or 'maxed out' the individual that is suing you can only go after the asset in the LLC that they were injured at.

Here is an example. John Dough and his wife are living at 2601 Hobson Street which is one of two homes which form the LLC known as "Red Dog LLC." Their Christmas tree catches on fire, the house burns down and their daughter dies of smoke inhalation. A jury finds you had a faulty outlet and awards the Doughs $3 million. "Red Dog LLC" only carries $1,000,000 liability policy. What happens now and who is responsible for the other $2 million? Not you, thanks to your good friend LLC. Nobody is responsible for the money and one million dollars is the only cash award the Doughs will be receiving. They can demand that the other assets in Red Dog be sold, but they will not be able to place liens on your primary residence, "Blue Dog LLC," or "Yellow Dog LLC." They will not be able to sue outside the bubble of "Red Dog LLC." What's in "Red Dog LLC" is all they can get, the rest is yours to keep. Now instead of losing six rental properties and your primary residence due to a fire, you only lose two properties. After receiving your $50,000 fire policy check (you will receive the fire policy check, your name is on the insurance binder, not the Doughs) you're really only losing one. Sure, it still sucks. Anytime you lose something, it sucks, but it could have been a lot worse if you hadn't formed an LLC. Time will pass, you'll make more money, buy more properties, and you will soon forget about the property you lost. Shit happens, just make sure you're covered when it does.

The paragraphs above were my thoughts and views on what an LLC is and how it works. I hope you found it interesting, easily understandable, and most importantly helpful. The writings below are from Jim Bennett.

First, Nick and I would like to thank Jim for allowing us to use his valuable information in our book. Thanks Jim, we appreciate it and so will anybody who reads this section. Although you will find Jim's explanations a bit more involved than mine, I find it easy to understand and they are packed with a ton of useful info.

I've talked to people about LLCs and corporations. I've read numerous books and guides on LLCs and corporations. Hell, I've even purchased tapes and CDs on LLCs and corporations. I got more out of these next 12 pages than all of the above combined. Save yourself the time, money, and headaches and just read the following chapter. They're gonna tell you everything you need to know: start-ups, benefits, drawbacks, tax information, corporate fringe benefits, estate planning, etc. You name it, it's in there. I'm going to give it to you the exact same way Jim gave it to me. So here it is, read it, learn from it, and enjoy it.

Diversified Real Estate Investor Group

AN INTRODUCTION TO THE LLC

By James M. Bennett

February 26, 2005

Disclaimer - The author intends to provide accurate and authoritative information with regards to the subject matter covered However it is offered with the understanding that the author does not engage in the rendering of legal, accounting or other professional services- If legal, accounting, tax. or other expert advice is required, the reader should retain the services of a competent professional. This information is for instructional purposes only. Readers should proceed with caution and seek the advice of hired professionals before implementing any of the strategies contained herein.

1. What is an LLC? The Limited Liability Company is a hybrid. A general partnership in structure and style of management with the general partners having personal limited liability. Or a limited partnership where the limited partners have management rights. Management and tax benefits of a partnership, liability protection of a corporation, with no need for the formalities of a corporation.

2. Benefits of an LLC

   - Full personal liability protection for owners and managers
   - Financial privacy
   - A separate legal entity - different from owners.

- Quick, cheap, and easy to step-up
- Few- corporate formalities.
- Asset protection benefits of a limited partnership - charging order
- Owners may be any legal entity or even foreigners, unlimited number of owners
- Flexibility in the allocation of profits and losses - not necessarily prorated
- Taxes - may file its own return, or not (only if single person)
- Tax year selection - Calendar or fiscal (usually calendar).
- May elect to be taxed as either a partnership or a corp. - "check the box"
- No double taxation of dividends.

3. Drawbacks of an LLC.

- A new type of entity - little case law. Not tried and true like corp. or L.P
- Lack of accounting and legal expertise.
- Existence not perpetual like a corporation - in most states 30 year existence
- Dissolution upon death or withdrawal of an owner (Note • may be reorganized by the election of the surviving members)
- In PA - subject to state corporate income taxes - the big drawback!
- Another set of books and accounts to keep.

- Will limit the type of real estate financing available.

4. What is Needed to Set Up an LLC?

- Certificate of Organization (in some States • Articles of Organization).

- Operating Agreement - similar to a partnership agreement.

   (Note - high!) recommended, but if single person LLC, may not be needed

- Certificate of Ownership - optional.

- Company Seal - optional.

- SS-4 Form - Request for Employer Identification Number (EIN) - maybe.

- Tax Forms - Federal - Usually a Partnership 1055 Form or a Corp. 1120 Form

- Tax Forms - State - PA 65 (Partnership Return) & PA RCT - 101 (Corp. Tax Return)

5. What Is a "Member"?

A Member is an owner of interests in an LLC (membership interests). The member has the rights to income and loss distribution on a pro-rata basis or as is specified within the Operating Agreement. The member has rights to participate in the management of the company as specified in the Certificate of Organization and/or Operating Agreement.

- In lieu of using the title "member", the LLC may elect to adopt corporate titles such as President, Vice President, Secretary, & Treasurer.

- Managing Members vs. Non-Managing Members - like General and Limited Partners.

- Lability - Neither members nor managers are personally liable for the debt, obligations or other liabilities or torts of the company solely by reason of being or acting as members or managers. Failure of the LLC to observe corporate formalities is not ground for imparting personal liability on the members or managers.

6. Member Managed vs. Manager Managed.

- Member Managed. In a member managed LLC, the owners, or members managed the company like general partners in a general partnership. Each has a vote in proportion to his/her S membership interest. All the owners more or less act as part of the Board of Directors or "Board of Members".

- Manager Managed. One or two Members are designated in the Operating Agreement as "active'" or "Managing Members". the others are designated as "passive" or "Non-Managing Members".

- Management Authority. Primarily by virtue of the Operating Agreement, but may abo be referenced in the Certificate of Organization.

7. The Operating Agreement. (Similar to a partnership agreement.) Items to consider.

  What is included?

- Name of the LLC

- Owners' names, addresses. % ownership and capital contributed.

- Owners' management responsibility, authority and compensation.

- Ownership "Buy/Sell" Agreement. Funded by life insurance?

- Valuation method used for "Buy/Sell"

- Methods of accounting. (Generally cash basis on a calendar year)

- Transfer of ownership and limitations therein. (Rights of first refusal?)

- Allocation of profits and losses

- Permitted and prohibited transaction

- Business goals and objectives and line of business.

- Selection of Bank. Accountant. Attorney

- Active vs. Passive Members - (Note SE Tax. pension implications)

8. Taxation of LLCs.

   - Single Person LLC - Can have or not have its own tax returns/ EIN.

   - Federal - "Check the Box" - default is as a partnership, but may elect taxation as a corporation.

   - State - most states tax as a partnership - NOT IN PA. Taxed as a corp.

- Estate Tax Implications - Step up in basis. With corporation, you may have capital gains tax issues within the corp. Not with an LLC.

9. Self-Employment Taxes and LLCs.

- In general, the distributive share of earnings from an LLC are subject to self-employment taxes. Taxes paid by the members being allocated the earnings

- "Guaranteed Payments" Term for compensation or services paid to a member within an LLC. Guaranteed payments are subject to S.E. tax.

- Election of "Active vs. Passive" In Operating Agreement. Managing members vs. non-managing. May be able to avoid S.E. tax based on situation.

- Nature of Income. Interest. Dividends. Rer.ts - passive. therefore, not subject to S.E tax? Some accountants say yes. others say no.

10. Distribution of Earnings in an LLC.

- In a Corporation - Pro-rata based on share ownership.

- In an LLC - However the panes agree to slice and dice it (usually defined in the Operating Agreement). Implications for high and low tax bracket members. (i.e. High tax bracket investors get more basis in the LLC (growth). Low tax bracket investors get distributions of taxable earnings.

- "In-Kind" Distributions - In a corp. deemed as a sale, therefore subject to capital gains. In an LLC - not deemed as sales, therefore, no capital gains, the person receiving the distribution gets property at the LLCs cost basis.

11. Writing off of Losses In an LLC.

- Subject to at risk limitations. In general, you can only take losses up to your basis in the LLC. plus the value of recourse debt. Once your basis is written down to zero, losses are suspended ard "carried forward" until the LLC has more earnings or is liquidated.

- Generally - if have passive losses - try to offset with passive income. If you have active losses, try to offset with active income

12. Withdrawal of Members. Upon the death or withdrawal of a member, the LLC must be dissolved. The surviving members may elect to reform the LLC. Note - this is dramatically different from c corp which survives the death of a shareholder

13. Estate Planning Issues.

- Gifting of minority interests to family members

- Use as a replacement to family limited partnership.

- Minority interest estate tax valuation discounts.

- Market value estate tax discount.

- Non-continuity after death - must have family member willing and able to reform and continue or at least wind-down the business.

14. Recommended Uses for the I.LC.

- In lieu of a sole proprietorship - any Schedule "C' activity

- In lieu of a general partnership.

- For buy. fix and flip deals. To separate cut "deal status'" from your other properties

- As a management company

- As a general contracting company.

- As a general partner in a limited partnership.

- As an entity in a "'multi-layered" transaction

15. Introduction to LLC Layering Strategies.

- A limited partnership (LP) owns the property. General partner is a corporation, with the individual investor as the limited partner.

- L.P. master leases to an LLC

- LLC deals with the tenant on a "sub-let " basis. LLC is contractually responsible for all maintenance, repairs, everything related to the property.

- LLC holds few if any assets

- Insulation of the property and the individual owner from most, if not all, liability.

- Individual investor is 2 layers removed from any tenant related liability, protected by the LLC and the LP.

CHAPTER 19

MISTAKES

MISTAKES WE MADE AND
WHAT YOU CAN DO TO PREVENT THEM.

Well, not to sound like a smartass, but if you read this book from front
to back you're going to prevent about 1,000 mistakes. Money saving
mistakes, time saving mistakes, financing mistakes, etc. That's right,
you name the category and we made the mistake! It's not that we were
two idiots, it's just that we didn't have any experience. That's what this
book is all about, an experience in the world of Section Eight Housing.
Nick and I lived it.

Sure, we both new things about plumbing, electric, painting, etc.
But dealing with Section 8 inspections and Section 8 tenants was a
totally different animal. It was something neither of us knew anything
about. Yet every day for the past 8 years we gained more and more
experience and knowledge.

I've heard people in this field say the experience of being a section 8 landlord is something you can't prepare for, you have to figure out and solve the problems as they come at you. My answer to that comment would be, "Bullshit!" Had I bought a copy of this book about 8 years ago I would have saved myself hundreds of thousands of dollars, about 10,000 hours of time and at least 1 million headaches! They say you can't buy experience, but I believe otherwise.

If a roofer said to me, "For five dollars, I'll tell you what to use on your roof."

I'd say "Okay, mister roofer, here's your five dollars. What do I use on my roof and why do I use it?"

"Use rubber, never hot tar. For an extra $200 your roof will last 3 times longer."

In my mind, I just bought experience. For five bucks you prevented yourself from making a costly mistake.

We learned by trial and error. At the time, there was no other way. We asked a ton of questions and came up with a ton of great ideas. If an idea worked, we added it to our repertoire and repeated it as much as possible. If it didn't, we scrapped it and tried something else. Never after trying something that didn't work, did we think we failed? We went by Thomas Edison's motto, "I have not failed, I just found 10,000 ways that didn't work."

I would be lying by saying that if you read this book, you won't make any mistakes. **You Will!** But the longer you stay in this field the mistakes will become fewer and far between. That's the point at which Nick and I are at now. Mistakes are not made on a regular basis, and when they do pop up we don't panic, we just figure out a way to make sure we don't make that mistake ever again. That's the point where I want to get you, the reader and purchaser of this book to. I don't want to sound like a car salesman, but I honestly believe that by reading this book you can truly save yourself hundreds of mistakes.

They say you learn from your mistakes, but be smart, learn from someone else's mistakes, Mike and Nick's! Eight years of mistakes wrapped up in one book. The bottom line is this, you're going to make mistakes. Everybody docs. Nick and I think we've got this section 8 rental business down to a tee. Will we make a mistake in the next week or two? Probably! Once you make a mistake, learn from it. Never lose another dime on this type of a mistake again. Next, I list our seven most crucial mistakes, and the ones we think will be most beneficial for you to know about. Whether something works out or doesn't work out, you've learned. Don't get discouraged. Try again and again until you get it right. Once you get it right, you'll never get it wrong again.

7 MISTAKES YOU DON'T WANT TO MAKE

1. Not creating an LLC — We didn't create any LLCs until we were about sixty houses deep into this business. We got lucky. We could have been sued and lost everything. Why didn't we do it? We didn't know anything about them. But now, you do. So, don't make the same mistake we did. Create an LLC and cover your ASS!

2. Not replacing old wooden windows — We did not replace the wooden windows when we first purchased a home. What happened? We failed many inspections for chipping paint, broken

177

window locks, windows that wouldn't go up, windows that wouldn't stay up, etc. Why didn't we change them? *We thought* we were saving money. Really, we were losing money. If your rent is $700 per month and you fail only two inspections over the lifetime in which you own the property due to your old windows, you just lost $1,400. Most rowhomes only have about 10 windows. A window costs $125. 10 x 125 = $1,250. By replacing your old windows, you would have saved $150 plus you would have had new windows to boot! Also, you would have increased your property's value. Don't be cheap with windows. Replace them. You will be good for the next 30 years.

3. Giving your tenants the okay to paint — We gave the tenants permission to paint if they wished. Ninety-five percent did not take us up on our offer. Thank God! The other 5% were color blind. Why did we let them paint? We figured that if they took the initiative to paint the place, maybe they would take care of the place. Never did we think they would paint the walls violet, pink, cherry, black cherry, etc. I think they got their color schemes from the side of a water ice truck. Never did we think that we would have to stain kill the wall 5 times before their colors would stop bleeding through. Never did we think they would ask us to replace the carpet because it has paint all over it! Say NO WAY to paint. The color that was on the wall when they moved in will be the same on the way out.

4. Not being present for your annual section 8 inspections — In the beginning we were not there when the inspector came out to do his inspection. Result – 80% of the time we failed. Why should you be there? To give yourself a fighting chance and to keep your tenants

big mouth shut. If you are present and the inspector finds a hole in the wall, he is going to write it up as a "tenant repair," you *will* still get paid. If you are not there, the tenant will more than likely say she does not know how the hole got there or that it was there when she moved in. Now, it becomes a landlord's repair. If you do not complete the repair in 30 days you **will not** get paid. If you are there and the tenant still opens her mouth (which probably will be the case) and says the hole was there when she moved in you will be able to: A) Tell her she is full of shit B) Show her a picture of how the wall looked before she moved in C) Make sure the inspector writes it up as a tenant repair D) All of the above. D would be the right answer. Being at all of your inspections is the most important part of trying to pass your inspections. Not only will you get an idea of how your tenant is treating your property, but you will also know exactly what the inspector needs you to do if there are any repairs needed. A bonus is that you may become friendly with the inspector. It's harder to fail a friend who is standing right next to you, than to fail a stranger who is not!

5. Leaving luxury items for your tenants to use — We call hoses, dishwashers, ceiling fans, washer and dryer hookups, garbage disposals, air conditioners, screen doors, etc. a luxury. Why are they tenant luxuries? You don't need them to pass inspection! It is something that will end up costing you money and it is something they can live without. Think about it. If they are getting their rent paid for free, why should you lose 2 cents repairing things they don't need. Cut 'em, Cap 'em, Eliminate 'em, Trash 'em. Do what

ya gotta do to get rid of everything you don't need to pass inspections.

6. Replacing Carpets — In the beginning we did it all the time. What happened? We continued to replace and replace. What changed? We found and invented inexpensive ways to dress up our floors. All were cheaper and outlasted carpet. If I had all the money back I wasted on carpet, I wouldn't be trying to make a buck off this book. The worst investment you can make in a rental property is carpet. Not to mention it is one of the most expensive. I know that sometimes there is no way around it, but if you figure one out, let us know. Maybe we will put you and your idea in our next book.

7. Giving your tenant your home or cell phone number — Our first six tenants received our home and cell numbers. Then we had to change them. The next five hundred or so tenants got the number to our secondary office number, which was hooked up to an answering machine. If you are looking for the fastest way to be committed into a mental hospital, go ahead and give all your tenants your personal numbers. Not only will they call you at 11 o'clock at night to tell you the kitchen light bulb blew out, but they will also call you at 4 o'clock in the morning to tell you it came back on. If you don't come over their property to fix a specific problem right away, be prepared for their 75-year-old mother to call you 55 times or their live-in boyfriend who shouldn't even be living at the property to call you. Whatever the case, let them talk to the machine. This way you can decipher what is important and what is not important. To hear them, everything is an emergency. You and your answering machine will be the judge of that!

CHAPTER 20

FINAL THOUGHTS ON SECTION 8 LANDLORDING

Throughout this book, Nick and I bitch, complain, and tell you about some of the nightmares and all of the problems we have encountered over the last eight years. Why do we only tell you the bad and not the good? Because good tenants don't cause problems. You really can't learn anything from a good tenant other than to let them be! There's nothing I can write about problem solving if I don't have any problems. It's the bad ones that make our blood boil. The ones you try to outthink and stay five steps ahead of. If I had all good Section 8 tenants, this book wouldn't make it to page 1. I would simply tell you to rent the house "as is." No need to eliminate anything, no need to take extra precautions, no need to do anything extra because your excellent Section 8 tenants will keep your property in excellent condition. Hell, waive the security deposit while you're at it.

Honestly, if Section 8 landlording was that easy, you wouldn't buy the book. You wouldn't need it. Everybody and their brother would be doing Section 8 housing. No, the Section 8 rental business is not that easy, but it does work and it is profitable. The better you get at it, the more profitable it becomes. Don't listen to the naysayers who tell you to "stay away" or "don't get involved." Chances are they never owned a property in their life let alone a Section 8 rental property. Eighty percent of our tenants were good or average, 10% were pains in the ass but tolerable, and the other 10% are the one's we're writing the book about.

The best thing Nick and I ever did was get involved with Section 8 housing and we knew it right away. Where else can you purchase a house for $20,000 and rent it out for $750 a month? If your tenant stays for a little more than 2 years, you just made all your money back. Try getting that kind of return at the bank or on Wall Street. We've had tenants for 5 or more years who we haven't heard from, yet they continue to pass inspections. They've paid the house off 2 times over and are going on their third. You also get three very important bonuses from being a Section 8 landlord that you don't get as a private landlord. These bonuses are huge!

#1 What appeals to me most is that I get paid on the first of every month. About 90% of my rent is guaranteed by the government and is wired directly into my bank account. I get dollars, not excuses.

#2 Tenant motivation – their motivation to pay any portion of their rent is that they know if they are evicted, they will lose their Section 8 packet. There's a Section 8 waiting list a mile long full of good tenants just waiting for the bad ones to screw up.

#3 Rules – sure, regular tenants have to follow rules also, but not as many as a Section 8 tenant. They must follow rules about nuisance, housekeeping, criminal activity, occupancy, and transparency. Loud music, fighting, late rent, poor housekeeping, drug use, not paying their utility bills all count against them. Once again, the motivation factor comes into play. If they don't follow the rules, they get evicted. If they get 3 community complaints, they lose their packet. If they get evicted, they kiss their Section 8 packet goodbye.

The system really works out well in most cases. When the bad cases come along, it's not the end of the world either. Get rid of the tenant, re-rent the home, and make sure the problem never repeats itself.

CHAPTER 21

WRAPPING IT UP

A Note from Mike on February 2020

Hey guys, it's Mike McLean here. I'd like to personally thank you for your purchase of the Section 8 Bible Volume 1. I hope you enjoyed it. I can't believe it's been 15 years since I first wrote it. Wow, time flew by so quickly! Anyway, let me tell you a little bit more about the book and how the whole Section 8 Bible series got started.

Volume 1 was a cool book to write and here's how it originated. Nick and I would be at a settlement table, closing on another house or at a friend's party just kicking back enjoying a couple of beers and we'd get into telling a story on what one of our crazy tenants did and what we did to retaliate. Well, no matter where or when we would tell these stories, people would be pissing themselves laughing and if I had a dollar for every time I heard, "You guys have got to write a book on this shit," I'd be filthy rich. So I did!

Now I didn't know the first thing about writing a book or how to get it published, or even how the hell to market it. I knew that if I could figure out the Section 8 game, then the book writing would be a breeze compared to that. So, I sat down at my dining room table every night and I started writing! To tell you the truth, I think I ripped up the first two finished drafts, they sucked!

I was trying to be intellectual and talking like a real estate professor rather than like myself. I'm no professor, I'm a Section 8 landlord! So after I read the drafts back, they came off as boring as a dry mop. This wasn't what people were laughing at, this wasn't the stuff people were begging to hear more stories about, this was shit! So the third and final time, I decided to write and talk like myself. I figured I'd tell it like it is and if nobody liked it or bought the book, oh well, at least I stayed true to myself.

Well guess what, the book took off! I'm so glad there are people out there like yourself who can still enjoy a book that might not be perfect punctuation wise, and have a curse word here or there, but are still able to learn from the book. Look, it doesn't take a rocket scientist to figure out how to explain that you won't learn anything from the second kick of a mule, and that's how easy I keep the lessons in my books. I have taken the kicks and put them into stories so that when you get involved, you won't get kicked!

Two years after releasing Volume 1, I released my next masterpiece, Volume 2! I was really comfortable with my writing style by now and I knew what I could get away with, so I pushed Volume 2 as far as I could push it. I really get down to the nuts and bolts of how to succeed and what to expect in the world of Section 8 Housing. I hope you'll come along with me on my journey and dive into Volume 2, I guarantee you that you'll enjoy it and continue to learn!

If Volume 1 was enough for you, I totally understand and, again, I thank you for your purchase. If possible, could you take a second or two to write a quick review on Amazon? I'd appreciate it.

If you decided to get involved in this game, I sincerely wish you good luck with your rentals. You can do this!

"THE GREATEST TOOL A LANDLORD CAN OWN IS AN AIRTIGHT LEASE"

After losing one too many eviction hearings, I realized that every lease I had purchased wasn't worth the paper it was printed on! So, I designed the Bulletproof Lease to protect me and my property.

My lease is packed with 41 terms and 14 addendums that protect you in easy-to-read English (so you won't have to worry about some fancy lawyer trying to use your words against you.) The addendums protect you more because the tenant must sign each and every one.

When I started out, I was using a lease that simply stated that the tenant would be responsible to replace any and all broken windows. Simple enough, right?

Wrong!

This one tenant had four broken windows that he refused to repair. His neighbors told me that his girlfriend had locked him out, and he went nuts. When I took him to court, the tenant claimed that kids playing baseball broke the windows—all four. Well, the judge bought the tenant's story and I was stuck with the tenant and the repair bill.

Now, my tenants must sign the "Broken Window Addendum." It's as simple as getting a signature, and I don't get any more broken window calls!

I'm currently using this exact lease on all 300 of my investment properties and I will never go back to a flimsy generic lease again.

I designed it, I use it, and I stand by it! It's your money and your investment, so play by your rules, not the tenant's! I guarantee that you will never think of using a generic lease again.

Get it at: www.shoptly.com/bulletprooflease

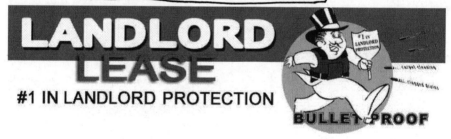

Other Titles

Section 8 Bible Volume II

Section 8 Bible Volume III

The Bulletproof Lease

Metal Money

Section 8 Secrets: Get Housing Assistance Faster

Made in the USA
San Bernardino, CA
24 March 2020